The INTUITIVE DETECTIVE

STACEY WEBB

Copyright © Stacey Webb

First published in Australia in 2022
by KMD Books
Waikiki, WA 6169

All rights reserved. No part of this book may be used or reproduced by any means, graphic, electronic, or mechanical, including photocopying, recording, taping or by any information storage retrieval system without the written permission of the copyright owner except in the case of brief quotations embodied in critical articles and reviews.

Because of the dynamic nature of the Internet, any web addresses or links contained in this book may have changed since publication and may no longer be vaild. The views expressed in this work are solely those of the author and do not necessarily reflect the views of the publisher and the publisher hereby disclaims any responsibility for them.

Cover design by Ida Jensson

Edited by Danielle Line

Typeset in Sabon LT Pro 11/15pt

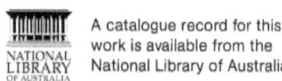

A catalogue record for this work is available from the National Library of Australia

National Library of Australia Catalogue-in-Publication data:

The Intuitive Detective/Stacey Webb

ISBN:
978-0-6454076-4-8
(Paperback)

ISBN:
978-0-6454076-5-5
(Ebook)

To my husband and four children, thank you for your unapologetically loving support and guiding me on writing this book as a step towards healing myself.

ACKNOWLEDGEMENT OF COUNTRY

I give thanks to the traditional owners of the land where The Intuitive Detective has chiefly been written (Sydney), the Dharug and Gundungurra people of the Ngurra Nation, and pay my respects to their elders, past, present and emerging.

AUTHOR NOTE

This book is a memoir. It reflects my recollections and opinions of experiences over time. Some names have been changed to protect the privacy of individuals.

CONTENTS

Introduction xi
Different types of intuition xiii

PART 1: FOLLOWING THE BREADCRUMBS 1
1 Fear of spiders falling on my head 3
2 This is your brother, Robert 5
3 Have a great day at school. I love you 7
4 Afraid to step through the door 9
5 Life after 12
6 Chocolate 14
7 Hey, what's your A/S/L? 16
8 Changing schools 18
9 Stop this study 20
10 Turn off your radio, charge your phone, and wind down your window 22
11 Finding out the truth 26
12 People pleasing 29

PART 2: LEADING TOWARDS MY PURPOSE 33
13 Are you okay? 35
14 Attestation day 38
15 The fear to seek help 40
16 Shots fired 43
17 We found the other two 47
18 Neighbourhood dispute 49
19 Christmas angel 53
20 Becoming a detective 55
21 Can I ask you a question? 57

22 Angel	60
23 Death message	63
24 Creating and holding space	66
25 Get out of here	68
26 Emotional rollercoaster	71

PART 3: SEEDS ARE PLANTED 75

27 I'm pregnant	77
28 Returning from maternity leave	80
29 Allanah	82
30 Turn off the life support	85
31 Warrior	87
32 Welcome to our home	89
33 Transition	91
34 He's gone, he's gone	93
35 Message received	96
36 I guess we're not buying that car today?	99
37 Hearing a scream when no one screamed	102

PART 4: WAKING UP TO MY POWER 107

38 You have a voice	109
39 Nothing needs to be fixed there	111
40 Releasing the guilt	113
41 Trauma in my body	116
42 Love yourself	119
43 A new way of thinking	124
44 Scaffolding	127
45 It's time to go deeper within your intuition	129
46 Shit magnet	131
47 A step forward	133
48 Spiritual closet	135
49 Sacred leader	137
50 My service is my medicine	139
51 Patterns	142

Writing this book	145
Acknowledgments	147
About the author	149

INTRODUCTION

This book is a story of my life, but with a different twist. It won't include every event that happened. It won't include every single traumatic event that happened. And it won't include all my police stories, with all the different jobs I've attended, arrests made, and court cases over the years either. This book will show how the different types of intuition have appeared in my life as a child, young adult, police officer, mother, and as an overall human being. And I know this will continue even after this book is complete. Not only the times I listened to my intuition, but the times I avoided or blocked my intuition, too. It shows how intuition can be subtle, and when you avoid it, it will keep trying to make its presence known.

As a mother to four children, including twins, who's worked as a police officer for fifteen years, a detective for thirteen of those years, and has a passion to assist people with trauma, I have a busy life. While I love taking some self-care for me and read books, it depends on the time I have available to not only read through a book but even just getting through a chapter. As such, I have created mini chapters within the chapters. It's a way for you to read with ease during your busy lives and still love this book.

DIFFERENT TYPES OF INTUITION

Before I go into my story of how intuition has guided me, it is important to know there are different types of intuition and different ways we can receive it.

First, intuition is innate within all of us. It is not unique, and it is not a special gift only certain people can possess. In fact, everyone can access and connect to their intuition if you are willing to receive. Intuition is a muscle. You need to work on it, develop it, and strengthen it until it becomes second nature to you.

The higher the levels of intuition accessed, the more frequency tuning your consciousness needs to receive the information. There will be many times you may never understand the reasoning, the final destination your intuitive guidance may give you. Receiving from your intuition is not about knowing the answers behind the guidance. That is your mind, your ego wanting to know. Therefore, the important thing to remember is your intuition will never steer you wrong, and the choice is always ours in deciding to listen to our intuition or to listen to our fear and/or ego. There is much science behind intuition, with research constantly evolving around it. The foundation to remember is, if we choose to listen to our intuition, we choose love. We choose love over fear, therefore we have access to our unlimited consciousness.

We receive our intuition through 'clairs', These clairs are clairvoyance (clear sight), clairaudience (clear hearing), claircognisance (clear knowing), and clairsentience (clear feeling). I know the way I receive my intuition is through by knowing within myself (claircognisance), followed by the feeling within my body (clairsentience), then hearing (clairaudience) and finishing with seeing (clairvoyance). No, I am not a psychic who can predict the future and/or see people who are deceased. The spirits of people don't come to me to help solve crimes either.

Using intuition and being a police officer goes hand in hand. Most people who contact and interact with police will be because of an underlying fear they have. Usually, a fear of the projected future and/or fear of the past. A police officer, without even realising it, will from time to time use their intuition when contacting and interacting with the public and I will explain over the different types of intuition how that can be.

The two main heads of intuition are local and non-local intuition.

The most known local intuition that people hear about is the 'gut instinct' or 'survival intuition', where a person can connect to their energetic sensitivity. Survival intuition alerts police officers to danger not just for themselves but to the public too. The activation of their 'gut instinct' and 'survival intuition' may occur when a police officer saves the life of another within a split-second decision or when they themselves are injured on the job yet still have the strength to continue to save the life of another.

Energetic sensitivity allows police officers to have an awareness of the archetypal energies they may encounter with a person so they can best communicate with them. This can occur just by a police officer walking in a room and feeling the energy that an argument recently took place. It can also occur when a police officer speaks with a person who wishes to self-harm to reconsider their choice and receive assistance through mental health avenues. It allows police officers to co-regulate another person's nervous system, such as speaking to a person who has just been stabbed. In trying to keep them calm whilst also giving first aid and/or obtain critical pieces of information as a person accesses their memory recall. This assists the investigation in obtaining specific information, allowing an offender to be identified.

Another local intuition phase is when a police officer can access implicit knowledge. When a police officer uses their experiences within the police, it becomes second nature to them. Being in the moment; subconsciously gaining an understanding and working through emotions, defences, and behaviours presented. This can come out to a police officer for things like knowing where to search in a car to find illicit drugs.

Or where to start a land scale search to locate a missing person. And how to ask certain questions for someone to feel safe enough to open themselves and disclose information that assists the investigation.

Creative intuition is another phase a police officer may access. However, it is more on a conscious level compared to the energetic sensitivity and implicit knowledge intuitions just mentioned. It is co-creative and therefore needs to be accessed and guided on without judgement or prejudice. This is where a police officer would act on the guidance and receive the information of where the investigation is taking them. Where a police officer tunes into their senses when speaking to victims, witnesses, and offenders if that is possible, and actively listens to what they have to say or don't say. It includes going through and testing what is available from your crime scene/s and/or exhibits, and presenting your criminal and/or coronial brief in a way that best presents all the information.

Non-local intuition is beyond local intuition. In its non-biological form, it doesn't contain any complicit knowledge and is purely all energy. Everything is energy, including us humans, and our energy expands more than our physical body because it interconnects us with everything.

It is what we are experiencing when we are attuned to our greater existence and network of consciousness. It cannot be defined by anything we've been taught and learnt. Inside non-local intuition is everything that exists in all times within the quantum field. We are innately intuitive intelligent beings and accessing non-local intuition is having the willingness to surrender without knowing some or all of the steps. A simple example could be a police officer out on patrol and choosing to drive down one street instead of another. Or choosing to drive down the street where your offsider turns around questioning why you drove down this road instead of the road you may normally take, because of your implicit intuition. And unbeknown to you, as you drive down the street you chose, a job is broadcasted on the radio and low and behold, you are on that same street. Another example is when a police officer may attempt a new way to obtain information legally within an investigation, ways that may not be commonly used or may be new to policing investigations. Surrendering; by following and receiving guidance of where the investigation leads and presents to them without judgement. This means the police officer must not lead or expect what their victims and witnesses will say in their statements to 'get the bad guy', or to 'win the court case' with their brief. It is investigating the matter at its highest potential with non-dualism.

PART 1
FOLLOWING THE BREADCRUMBS

1
FEAR OF SPIDERS FALLING ON MY HEAD

When I was eight, my mum was pregnant, and we were preparing for a new brother or sister. One night, when my mum was full term, she went to have a shower. Dad was working night shift, and I was in the kitchen. Not long after she went into the bathroom, I heard my parents' bedroom door slam shut. Within my body, I intuitively knew something was wrong.

I heard my mum yell out my name from the bedroom. I remember the tone within her scream as she yelled out my name. It was filled with panic, fear, and an attempt of masking it all with calmness to not alert me.

I immediately ran to the bedroom door and said, "Yes, Mum."

"Get Aunty Margaret," she replied in a hurried and scared voice.

We were all on alert for when Mum went into labour, but this seemed different. It seemed more serious, but I wasn't sure what was wrong. I ran out the front door and raced down the street. I didn't run out for excitement about the impending birth of my sibling. I ran because I knew something was seriously wrong.

One of my fears at that time of my life was walking under trees at night in case I walked into a spider web, or my worse fear, having a spider fall on me. Between my house and Aunty Margaret's house, there were no real walk paths nor a lot of streetlights. But I knew there was roughly one tree out the front of each house's nature strip that I would have to run under. I was scared. Scared of my fear of spiders and scared of my mum being in trouble with my baby brother or sister. It is the first memory I have of facing a fear within my life and how I chose the love of my mum and unborn sibling over everything else.

I ran along the nature strip to Aunty Margaret's house. I knew every bump in the grass, every large stone, and every little ditch to avoid. It was pitch black outside, and I was running just knowing the way within my body. I was preparing for a race I didn't know I was racing until this night. I didn't stop. I knew I couldn't stop until I got to Aunty Margaret's. The whole time I ran I just kept saying to myself, "I can do this."

I banged on the door as loudly as I could yelling, "Aunty Margaret." My hand hurt from using my fist to bang on the door with such urgency. Aunty Margaret came to the door in what felt like an instant after banging on her door.

"Your mum?" she said.

"Yes, quickly hurry," I replied.

Aunty Margaret took me home, and an ambulance arrived shortly after where my mum was taken to the hospital.

All I could feel within myself was that something was wrong, and it was urgent. I didn't know at the time, but when my mum called out to me from her bedroom, it was moments before she lost consciousness. My mum was bleeding internally with her and my sibling's life being in extreme danger.

> *The amazing thing is that we all have courage within us. Courage can be found in even the smallest of choices we make in our day-to-day life and doing them despite being afraid of it.*

2
THIS IS YOUR BROTHER, ROBERT

I remember walking in the hospital corridors and meeting my dad, who took me into a small room. I sat down on a chair and my dad said, "I have something to tell you. Mummy had the baby. It's a boy and his name is Robert. But sadly, Robert was born sleeping. It means, it means…"

As Dad was saying this, I could see he was getting upset. I could tell he was having trouble saying the words.

"It means Robert is in heaven now, doesn't it?"

"Yes Stacey," Dad replied. "It means Robert has died, and he is now in heaven."

The nurses brought us in to see Mum. My mum, who has dark olive skin, was as pale as pale could be. She was sitting in her hospital bed and was holding Robert, who was wrapped up in a muslin blanket in her arms.

"This is your brother, Robert," Mum said. "Would you like to hold him?"

I nodded, sat down, and they brought Robert over to me, where I held him in my arms. I saw what looked like the most beautiful baby I'd ever seen to be sleeping peacefully.

We had photographs taken of us all holding Robert. I still have photos of me holding Robert to this day. When I mentioned this to people growing up, particularly in my teen years, I would get responses on how they thought this was disturbing for them to hear this. All they thought when I mentioned my story was that when I was eight, I had a photo holding a dead baby. This made them feel uncomfortable and in their eyes was taboo.

I remember my mum's trauma of Robert's death greatly impacted her when she was pregnant with my sister two years later. We weren't allowed to get anything ready for our new baby brother or sister. We didn't know the gender during the pregnancy. My sister didn't even have a name for the first five days as no name was allowed to be prepared before the birth.

This was my first experience with death that involved a person, and after Robert's funeral, I don't remember him being spoken about much growing up. Not until I became a young adult and became unafraid of people's reactions. Robert's death made me keenly aware of how much people fear death, especially a baby/child death. Fear that death and grief invite us to think, reflect, feel, and ask questions. Robert didn't breathe air in this life, but his soul was alive and still had a life experience whilst in the womb. What we tend to forget when we don't talk about death is that we stop talking about life.

> *It seemed people found it difficult to know what to say to me regarding Robert's passing. I knew and could feel they were uncomfortable in participating in a conversation or approaching the subject when it involved anything relating to Robert. But I didn't need advice or fixing. I just needed acknowledgement of Robert's existence and to feel seen and heard in times I needed to talk about him.*

3
HAVE A GREAT DAY AT SCHOOL. I LOVE YOU

When I was twelve and in Year 7 at high school, my dad was working in the warehouse after he took a redundancy from a beer company. Dad would sometimes carpool with other workers, as I would often hear the tooting of the horn from out the front yard. Dad would run through the hallway, getting his bag, and kissing me on the forehead before he went out the front door.

Two weeks before Christmas was scheduled to be a busy day. I had school and was playing finals in a school sport. I don't remember the sport other than it was a ball sport like tee ball or softball. However, I remember being worried and expressing to Dad about this because I wasn't good at ball sports and was worried I would have to catch the ball and I'd drop it. Also, in the afternoon through to the evening, I had the full dress rehearsal for our dancing school's end-of-year concert. While I was at school, my mum would finish sewing dancing costumes, not only mine but others, with my youngest sister, Lisa, two, in tow.

On this morning, I heard the horn tooting out the front. I looked out the window and saw a car take off. But I didn't hear the front door. Did my dad leave to go to work? I knew Mum was in her sewing room, as I could hear the sewing machine humming away. I knocked on the front door of my parents' bedroom and entered. Dad was lying in bed and the room was completely dark.

"Dad," I asked, "are you going to work today?"

"No Stace. I have a migraine coming along," Dad replied.

I remember Dad getting a lot of migraines where he needed to be in his bedroom with the curtains drawn so it was pitch black. I also remember he had insomnia, and it went hand in hand with his migraines.

"Okay. I will let you get some rest. I hope your migraine goes away soon," I said.

"Thank you," Dad said.

As I went to shut the bedroom door, Dad said, "Oh wait. Today you have your sports final, don't you?"

"Yea, I do. I'm really nervous in case I can't catch the ball," I said.

"You will do great, Stace. Have a great day at school. I love you," Dad said.

"Thanks, Dad. I love you too. I hope your migraine goes today."

I shut the bedroom door, and I left to go to school. I felt nervous all day. On edge and unfocused. I put it down to being nervous about playing in the sports day, but even after playing in the sports final and winning, the feeling within me didn't ease.

That morning, that conversation, that feeling, used to haunt me. Haunt me not only in my dreams but also whilst I was awake. To be honest, on some days it still carries its emotional charge. I now know that it's okay and more importantly, I now know there was nothing I could have done to change the events of that morning.

4
AFRAID TO STEP THROUGH THE DOOR

When I finished school, I expected to see my mum or dad ready to pick me up to get ready for the dress rehearsal for my dancing Christmas concert. The feeling of being on edge, unfocused and uneasy, was still there. When I walked out, I saw another family member, my uncle, waiting for me instead. My uncle was gazing over the heads of school students pouring out, trying to look for me. It took him time to see me, yet I picked him straight away. I instantly knew as I walked towards him that someone had died.

I questioned my uncle why he was picking me up.

He just replied, "They asked me to pick you up," and deflected answering anything else. I didn't believe him. I was at first offended he would think I would believe him.

As I got into the car, I asked myself in my mind, "Who has died? Mum, Dad or Lisa?" I put on my seatbelt. I knew and felt the answer to that question. "Dad." My heart sank and my stomach felt like I had several huge rocks weighing me down. I didn't say much during the car ride home. The feeling in my body was making me sick, and every time I looked at my uncle, he would look away and appear to concentrate on driving. I could feel and sense he was in grief, too.

As we got to my house, I saw several cars parked outside. "Why are there all these cars parked outside our house?"

"We're having a party," he said nervously back.

I knew this was a lie and again was even more offended he would think I would believe it. But that feeling only lasted a few seconds. 'He doesn't want to tell me,' was the reply I felt within. And so the following feeling I had for my uncle was compassion.

I walked to the front steps of my house and I stood still.

"Come on inside, Stacey."

I heard my uncle speak, however, I refused to move. I just stood there, looking at the front door of our house. The front door was open, but I was frozen, still in fear. I didn't want to walk through that front door. I knew if I walked through that front door, my intuition was correct. They'd tell me my dad was dead, and my life would change forever. I feared I would be right.

Mum appeared at the front door. I could see she was upset. Her eyes were puffy and red, and she had patches of red blotches all over her neck. She tried to put on a brave face.

Mum took a deep breath and asked, "Why won't you come inside Stacey?" in a careful way to not start crying herself.

"Because as soon as I walk through the door, you're going to tell me that my dad is dead," I said.

I burst into tears and tried to move, but my feet felt glued to the ground. I was still frozen in fear. I could not believe I said my thoughts out loud. Mum came out to me, she held me and cried with me in validation.

"No, no, no, please don't say that it is true," I just kept saying out loud as Mum walked me inside and into the lounge room.

"I'm sorry, sweetie, but it is true. Dad died today."

I let out a massive howl, clinging to my mum, and kept saying, "No, no, no, no." After what felt like an eternity but would have only been minutes, I said, "Was it his fault?"

"No Stacey, it wasn't his fault," Mum replied.

I lay in my bed in the foetal position, clinging to a teddy bear, and cried. Through my bedroom walls, I could hear other people's cries from all areas of the house and yard. People who gathered after hearing the news to be together.

I still didn't know how Dad died. After I emerged from my room and cried on the lounge as more people poured into our house, I overheard Mum say to someone on the phone Dad got electrocuted at the house. I walked up to Mum after she got off the phone. "Is that how Dad died?"

"Yes Stacey," Mum replied.

> *Knowing my dad died before I was told scared me, and I became fearful of my intuition, which in return created subconscious fear programs within me.*

5
LIFE AFTER

Life after Dad's death was different. I never saw any electricians come by the house. I mean, if someone were electrocuted, you would think an electrician would come. And if I were not at the house when the electrician was there, I would have eventually known about it.

I wanted to ask what happened to Dad. I didn't believe the electrocution story, but I was in fear of asking. In fear of learning the truth. I didn't want any more bad news and so I never asked. I abdicated my responsibility and felt it was easier not knowing. Each time I thought about it, or had questions, I always dismissed it. Pushed it deep down inside me and hoped it would not rise again. Over the years, Mum would ask me a subtle question about wanting to know a detail about Dad's death. I guess it was her way of wanting to tell me something, to reveal the secret. But the fear of the unknown, the fear of knowing I would be upset with whatever was said overruled everything else. And so, I always said no, I didn't want to hear anything. I was dismissing my intuitive thoughts on wanting to know more, believing it was easier not knowing. No matter the different ways my intuition tried to get my attention about this, I would avoid or hide it away again.

Although death was present within our family. It also was never spoken about much either. Birthdays and the date he died were significant days for me. However, I don't remember if we ever did anything about those days. I don't have any memory of this between the ages of twelve and seventeen.

I believe it was a part of my resistance to knowing more mixed with trauma. Because when it came to my father and his death, avoiding my intuition remained for most of my teenage life.

6
CHOCOLATE

The puberty years were tough, especially after Dad's death. My mum worked as much as she could, being a sub-contractor seamstress, and a lot of responsibility fell on me being the eldest to help around the house. This wasn't intentional, it was just how it was, and I believe the responsibility made me into the strong, determined, and courageous woman I am today.

Everyone else, from family members to parents of friends, loved having their opinion and telling me I needed to help around the house because I was the eldest. I needed to be a good girl and that meant doing what was asked of me without question. They would say this without even knowing the help I was already doing, and always just expected more from me. To me, they just floated in, said their piece to make them feel good, then floated away again. I had moments where I resisted sometimes, especially when I felt like I had enough or needed a rest. But most of the time I understood our family unit needed to stick together, and I just did what I had to do to help.

What helped me so much was having a job outside of school hours. When I was fourteen, there was a specialty chocolate store in the same shopping centre as my dance school. They had a notice on their shopfront for a junior worker to work Thursday nights and weekends. One of the dancing mums saw the sign and told my mum and me, thinking it would be perfect for me. As soon as I heard this, I thought of a memory I had with Dad when he was alive.

I remember my dad and I walking in the same shopping centre. As we were walking, I was asking Dad questions about why he worked night shift. Dad worked night shift in a beer factory before they made him redundant, and at that stage, I thought all jobs could only be worked during the day. Dad was saying how he loved working at the beer factory and he loved getting a discount for his beer.

"What would you love to have a discount on if you had to buy something, Stace?" Dad asked.

"I love chocolate," I said.

"So do I. Imagine one day if you worked in a chocolate shop? Imagine how much yummy chocolate we could eat," said Dad.

"That would be awesome. If I worked in a chocolate shop, I would spend my money on buying chocolate for everyone in our family. We can eat chocolate together," I said, squealing with excitement at my idea.

Dad started laughing and said, "Well, not every pay you get, maybe just your first pay."

When I was told about the chocolate store job, I knew I had to work there, and I knew I would get the job. I remember being so scared to even apply, but before I stepped inside the chocolate store for my interview, I stopped, took a deep breath, and thought, 'I have this job.' I was so excited when I found out I got the job. With my first paycheck of $19.87, I spent it on chocolates within the store for my family. As we all ate the chocolate together, I felt such a warm and calming sensation within me. I was happy.

So much sadness and grief surrounded most conversations involving my dad after his passing. Therefore, I love having stories like this to share. Because there were so many beautiful and happy moments we could easily miss or forgot to speak about.

7
HEY, WHAT'S YOUR A/S/L?

When I was fourteen, we got the internet for the first time in our house. Good ole dial up internet. It was supposed to be for homework purposes, and I was so excited. I went into a chat group on Australia Yahoo Chat to see what the chat rooms were all about. It was before online dating even became a thing. At that age, dating wasn't even on my radar. I was just excited to speak to someone on the other side of the world. Boxes would pop up on my screen from people wanting to chat to me. It was all overwhelming. There was one box that popped up from F.I.G.J.A.M. saying, "Hey, what's your a/s/l?" I ignored all the other chat requests and began chatting to F.I.G.J.A.M.

"What is a/s/l? I replied.

"Age/sex/location," F.I.G.J.A.M. wrote back. "I am 15/m/melb, u?"

"14/f/syd," I wrote back.

We chatted for ages and F.I.G.J.A.M. told me his name was Grant. We were in the same year at high school, and he described himself as 'an Aussie bogan.' I also found out what F.I.G.J.A.M. meant being 'Fuck I'm Good Just Ask Me.' When it was time for me to go offline, Grant asked, "Want to chat on MSN another time?"

"What's MSN?"

After Grant helped me set up MSN messenger, we both said goodbye. Over the years, we chatted on MSN to each other, and we became good friends. Talking on MSN messenger moved to talking and texting on the phone. When I was sixteen, Grant's family forgot to get him a present for Christmas. Grant told his parents to let him go to Sydney for a week during the January school holidays as his Christmas present where he can stay with his uncle who lived in the next suburb to me.

And that is what happened. Grant and I got to meet for the first time. We had never seen each other's face before. Mobile phones couldn't send picture messages back then. Wow! I felt older just writing that.

When I first saw Grant, I thought he was unbelievably cute. We had a great time catching up every day, and when my mum met him for the first time, she even invited him over for dinner the next night. And she cooked a roast dinner too. I initially lied to Mum about how I knew Grant. Sorry, Mum. Worried whether she would be angry and embarrassed for not telling her earlier. But I knew my intuition about my friendship with him was right and knew it would all be okay when she knew the truth.

Grant and I continued our friendship. We purely had a friendship where he had his girlfriends, and I had my boyfriends over the years. We would chat all the time with each other, and we knew everything about each other.

When I was eighteen, I had a surprise birthday party and Grant even travelled to Sydney as a surprise. A year later, Grant moved to Sydney, and not long after, we started dating and have been together ever since. Following the breadcrumbs that lead me to the Australia Yahoo Chat room and respond to his chat box asking for my a/s/l has led to finding the most incredible man.

> *It's a reminder to myself that although intuition is immediate and instant, it does not always give you the answer at the time, and you don't have to know the answers either. It may just be guiding you towards something else where you follow the breadcrumbs. In my case, it was becoming friends with Grant that evolved and grew into being in love with Grant, resulting in building a life together with our children.*

8
CHANGING SCHOOLS

I knew I wanted to be a police officer since I was fourteen. It was a feeling within me, a knowing it would be something I needed to do, something I wanted to do, something I knew would be a way to help people, and something I would be great at. I remember having arguments with my mum over the years about my desire to have a career in policing. Mum was initially not supportive, and we would often argue over it. She worried I would get hurt or worse, killed, whilst working on the job. She tried to use her fear of me joining the police force to overshadow my love for wanting to join.

When I was in Year 10, I was asked to think of what I wanted to study for my Higher School Certificate (HSC). The subjects you chose for your HSC helped mould what you would like to continue study in some sort of tertiary education, if that were the road you chose, after high school.

I always had a passion for legal studies and knew this would help me if I wanted to be in law enforcement. And so, at the end of Year 10, you would pick your subjects, and if there was enough interest in the study you'd chosen, they would hold the subject for you to study for the HSC.

Well, the time came at the end of Year 10 for the subjects that would be available for study in Year 11. Legal studies were not on it. Not enough students chose it. I was devastated. Teachers and friends told me to just choose another subject as 'it wasn't a big deal.' But even the thought of that didn't sit well with me. It didn't align with me.

"What will you do?" asked a friend.

"Simple, I will just change schools."

I researched and found the local high school closest to me was having legal studies as an HSC subject. There were student spaces, and I knew if I applied to transfer, I could study Legal Studies.

So, I went to my mum and told her I would change schools to study the subject most important to me. I don't even think I gave her a chance to object, but she supported the change anyway.

Looking back, I cannot believe I was so confident in what I wanted. I knew deep inside me I needed to do this. It was my intuition telling the knowing within me to do this. I knew this was what I wanted to do and so I did it. I had so much confidence and was so happy to go out of the unknown to make it happen. The love of studying what I wanted outlived the fear I had of going to a new school and not knowing anyone. I think my mum hoped I would choose to be a lawyer instead of a police officer. But alas, it was my intuition leaving me the breadcrumbs towards working on something greater in life.

It's easy to reflect on our lives and wonder how we had the strength and courage to do something. The thing is, we still have the strength and courage within us. Maybe our limiting beliefs and ego are coming in loud and strong.

To remember your strength and courage within, focus on your breath. With your fingers or whole hand on your heart centre, allow your breath to deepen. Deepening your inhales and exhales, allow your exhale to be slightly longer than the inhale.

This allows you to self-regulate your nervous system. It may take a moment, or several minutes of doing this until you feel safe within your body – open and connected to your heart/brain.

You can then feel the strength and courage within you that you felt was lost or didn't exist. It is still there, waiting for you to listen.

9
STOP THIS STUDY

At seventeen, I completed my Higher School Certificate (HSC), which is the last year of school. The requirement to join the police academy was a minimum age of eighteen, and you had to be nineteen to attend the police academy, where you are given the rank of Probationary Constable. I was too young. And the decision was made on what else I could do to fill in the year before I could go down to the police academy.

I thought about what type of police officer I wanted to be, and it led me to the thought of being a forensic police officer. Okay great, I will study Forensic Science then go into the police academy. This will give me the advantage of being accepted in Forensic Services within the Police Force after I do my minimum three years as a general duties police officer.

But to get accepted in forensic science at university meant I needed to reach a certain University Admission Index (UAI) mark. I received my UAI mark, and it wasn't at the required mark. In fact, it was quite lower than I expected. From memory, it was fifty-three point something. Just over the 'pass' mark. Thankfully, because I received high marks during my HSC throughout the year, a nearby university invited me to do some exams, which gave me a different mark. It was like a UAI and if this mark was higher than your UAI, you could use this mark to apply to any of their courses at that specific university. The mark I received from the university was much higher. It was in the eighties from memory, however, I was just a few points shy to do forensic science.

Resilience kicked in. No problems, I thought. I will just do a different course. It was suggested I do another science degree as that would help me and I was accepted to study Applied Science (Biological and Chemical Technologies). I also applied and was accepted in several T.A.F.E. courses to do Human Resources.

I was tempted to do the T.A.F.E. course in Human Resources. However, it seemed like everyone around me was so fixated on being accepted to the science degree.

"Why would you want to do a T.A.F.E. course when you can do a university course and it is in science?" is a comment I remember.

I was so caught up in receiving acknowledgement and validation on being accepted into a science degree, that they thought I was intelligent and were proud of me, that I accepted to study the science degree instead.

Even throughout my first year studying the science degree, I felt weird. I knew this wasn't the course for me. I started hating going to university, but receiving the validation from others, especially my mum being proud of me, kept me going. I would bring up the fact of still wanting to join the police force and would often get the response, "Why be a cop when you can do something more after having this degree? Something that can pay more money. Something that is safe."

Money didn't bother me. I always worked hard for my money and so I was happy to continue doing that as my career, as long as it was something I loved and enjoyed doing.

I continued to study the science degree even though everything inside me was saying "Stop this study." My intuition was telling me not to do this study. But I wasn't listening.

> *People-pleasing often leads to wanting to be chosen, validated, and loved. It may be whilst you are still trying to obtain it, that when you finally achieve it, you then realise you still don't feel whole. Not staying authentic to yourself and betraying yourself does not allow you to feel whole and complete within.*

10
TURN OFF YOUR RADIO, CHARGE YOUR PHONE, AND WIND DOWN YOUR WINDOW

I had about a year to go until I completed my science degree, and I was miserable with my life. I dreaded going to university and would often think of ways that could prevent me from attending like a car accident. It was weird. But I always wanted it to not involve another car as I never wanted anyone else to be injured or have their car damaged because of me being involved in the car accident. To be clear, I didn't want to die.

After being out with friends, I was driving home. It was nighttime and there was a large portion of my drive that included a long and winding single lane road and no streetlights. I'd driven this route many times, for not only seeing my friends but to attend university, too.

As I approached the turn off that started the single lane, no streetlights, with an abundance of large trees beside the road, inside me said, "Turn off your radio."

I had my music of Top 40, '00' music blaring and thought, "Yea, I better turn my music off," so I did.

Inside me then said, "You better put your phone on charge."

I looked at my phone and saw it had a charge of 90%. "I have plenty of charge. But okay, there is no harm in putting my phone on charge," and so I did and tucked my phone in the centre console of my car.

Inside me then said, "Wind down your window."

Why do I need to wind down my window? I hate driving with my window down. It's nighttime, and I am not feeling hot in the car.

I initially resisted, however, the nudge within me was strong, so I wound down my window.

Here I am parked on the side of the road, with my radio off, phone on charger, and driver's window wound completely down. I then set myself driving on a long and windy road with no streetlights. Many considered this tree-lined road one to pay attention to when driving, especially in the dark.

Halfway through, as I was approaching another bendy part of the road with a small bridge and creek underneath, I saw something dark dart across the road in front of me. I didn't know what it was and assumed it was an animal. There were kangaroos around this area, also dogs and even other farm animals from neighbouring farm properties. Whatever it was, it scared me, and my inexperienced driving instantly made me use my brakes. I pushed on my brakes hard and fast.

I lost control of my driving. As I tried to correct my steering, in a panic, I oversteered and veered off the road. As I mentioned, along this stretch of road there are large and tall trees along the whole road, except this small patch, which was where I veered off the road.

In this patch of grass that had no trees were two large piles of asphalt a metre high. I knew I would hit them. And I knew I could not stop it. I took a deep breath and instead of holding it, I let the breath out and breathed in again before I hit one pile of asphalt. My car, with me in it, flipped. The sound of my car crumbling around me as I was turning from the flip scared me and I was screaming from fear of being crushed. The car did a complete 360 with different parts of my car hitting either the pile of asphalt, the ground, or both along the way. I then hit the second asphalt pile and I continued screaming. I knew I was coming up to the creek and was so afraid I would roll into it and drown. My car rolled for the second time after hitting the second asphalt pile and my car landed on the roof, a metre away from the creek.

When my car stopped moving, resting on its roof, I also stopped screaming. I was upside down in my car. I thought, 'Okay, I need to get my phone to call for help.' I look in my centre console and my phone is not there. During the car rolling, it moved.

"Where is my phone?"

My phone then made a sound. I received a message from Grant wondering what I was up to. As I look in the front passenger well of my car, following the sound of the message tone, I saw my phone screen light up at the same time. When I tried to move to reach my phone, I realised I was stuck. My right arm was outside my driver's window and my hand was on the roof. Which meant the roof of my car was resting on my hand. Amongst the chaos of my car flipping, I didn't realise my arm was outside the window. Now I was stuck, and I couldn't move.

But my phone was still on the car charger. With my left hand, I followed the curly chord of my phone charger. I used it to bring in my phone to me by doing small pullbacks on the phone charger with my one hand to bring it closer towards me. At the same time, not pulling back on the charger too hard otherwise it will pull out of the phone and stay forever out of my hand's reach.

I brought in my phone using my phone charger and I called 000 to get an ambulance. At this time, I felt the pain of my hand that was stuck. I closed my eyes and started deep breathing again. Inhaled and exhaled with no holding of the breath before an inhale and no holding of the breath after an exhale. I didn't know it then, but I was doing conscious connected breathing. And as I breathed, I pressed the brake every time I exhaled. This helped me calm myself down.

As I am on the phone to the ambulance officers, giving them directions on how they can get to me, I hear two male voices approaching me. "Hello, is anyone there?"

"YES!" I screamed. "I'm here, I'm stuck. Please get me out."

Two young guys came out from nowhere. "Are you okay?" one said.

"My hand is stuck."

As one male walked closer towards me he said, "Yea, your hand and wrist is under your car. We should call an ambulance."

"I have called the ambulance already. I'm on the phone to them now. Please just turn this car over so I can get out."

By this point, I could not feel my hand anymore.

"What about your back or spine?," the other male said walking around to me.

"Look, the only thing that is hurting is my hand that my car is now on. And now I can't feel my arm. Please turn this car over," I said in a stern voice.

"Okay," both said with no argument.

My car, being a two door Hyundai Excel, meant it was a small car and thankfully, they both turned it over. Once I was sitting upright, I took off my seatbelt and climbed out of my driver's window because of both the driver and passenger doors being stuck.

"Wow," one guy said. "There is an indent where your hand was."

"How did you even find me? This street is pitch black."

"We saw your brake lights. It just kept going on and off in sequence and it caught our attention," one guy replied.

By this time, police and ambulance officers had turned up. I thanked these guys, who would have been eighteen to twenty years old, and off I went to hospital.

My mum and some friends came to the hospital to see how I was and unbeknownst to me, they also contacted Grant. Grant and I were still just friends at this point and lived in different states. However, Grant was so worried he was about to book a flight to see me. I assured Grant I was okay, and he didn't need to come up.

My hand and wrist were thankfully not injured too much because of this car accident. Just a sprain. By listening to my intuition of turning off my radio, putting my phone on charge, and winding down my window, these actions saved me. By listening to my intuition before driving down that road, I minimised this accident to a degree, being my injury and having no one else involved.

Several people said my dad was looking out for me that day. But what I believe was that I was listening to my intuition. And the talk of my dad looking out for me then started me thinking of him more, to question his death, and I felt ready to learn more. Again, this was my intuition guiding me and this time I was listening and following the breadcrumbs.

> *Of course, I learned a lot in the 3D world as well. I got a loan to buy another car and also received an infringement notice, a ticket from the police for negligent driving. I learnt big lessons about money management because of this car collision.*

11
FINDING OUT THE TRUTH

After my car accident, I borrowed my mum's car and took the train to university. I still hated studying this science degree. My heart just wasn't in it. But I continued to please others.

"You only have a year to go, Stace. You may as well finish it then do what you want to do," people would say.

A year is a long time. I was in my twenties and wanting to enjoy life, but I felt weighed down by wanting to please everyone else instead. I was out of alignment.

Being out of alignment also made me not listen to my intuition. If you remember from earlier, I thought if I had a car accident, it would then help make the decision to stop studying my science degree. Although it made me open my eyes to other things, the car accident and the breadcrumbs that led from that was what I believe to be a specific lesson for me. A lesson to not people-please and do what I wanted.

The months after my car accident weren't only the best feeling of my life, but also the worst. Something inside me kept wanting to know more about my dad's death. This troubled me at first because after he died, even though I knew things didn't add up to how he died, I still could not face the fear of knowing. I guess as the years went on, I became comfortable with the notion of not knowing. I was in my own little bubble, and if I desired to know more, I worried on how it would affect my life. I knew knowing about my dad's death would mean change. What I didn't realise was, I was so fearful of the unkown and change, that it was holding me back. I didn't like the life I was living, and my intuition was trying to tell me that YES, this will change your life, and changing your life is not a bad thing.

After denying my knowing regarding my dad's death, I finally got the courage one day to ask my mum the truth. I knew it was time to face my fear and walk through the darkness of going through the death of my father again. It was time to walk through the front door knowing my life would change forever. My mum sat down on the bed next to me, put her hand on mine, and said, "Stacey, your father killed himself."

I started crying, and I was crying on so many levels. I cried because I finally knew the truth, I cried because I was in denial on the truth. I cried because I realised my intuition was correct, that inside me always knew what I was told about how he died wasn't correct, and I cried because I was grieving all over again for my dad.

"But on the day he died, I asked you if what he did was his fault and you said no," I sobbed.

"And I wasn't lying there," she answered. "Your father wasn't well when he made the decision to end his life. I will always miss your father. He thought it was his only way out. Although it wasn't his fault, I always wished he knew there was another way for him to get better and still be here with us."

I asked a lot of questions and my mum patiently answered everything she knew, which included showing me the witness statement she made to police. I learned on the day my dad died, he decided to not go to work because of his migraine and inability to sleep. Whilst my mum was in her sewing room finishing one of my dance costumes for the dress rehearsal we had that night, he came in with some rope asking, "What is this rope for."

"It's for Stacey's costume," Mum replied.

"Oh, okay," Dad said as he walked away.

I remember Mum saying we never had rope at the house, so it wasn't an unusual question for him to ask where the rope came from.

Mum and my youngest sister, then two, went out to the shops to get something. Dad declined to go. When they returned, Mum saw my dad hanging from the rope I used with my dancing costume around his neck from the kitchen window. My heart sank hearing this, and again reading it in the police statement. I let out a big howl followed by uncontrollable sobbing as I learned my dad chose to die by suicide.

"Why did you tell us he was electrocuted?" I asked in between my sobbing.

"Because I couldn't bear the thought to tell you all the truth. I was trying to protect you kids." As Mum hugged me she said, "There were so many times I thought you were going to find out."

"What do you mean?" I replied.

"You questioned a lot of things, little things, even down to why he was wearing a collared shirt at the viewing before his funeral," Mum said.

I remember that moment of viewing my dad to say goodbye before his funeral.

"Yes, I remember now. I asked why he was wearing a collared shirt when I had never seen him wear one," I replied.

My dad was a singlet top and footy shorts kind of man and working in a factory meant he was wearing pants and a hi-vis shirt, never a collared shirt. My mum hung her head down.

As she wiped away her tears she said, "That was the best shirt I could find to cover the marks on his neck."

I realised by not facing this fear earlier in my life I was experiencing the pain of my father's death but was also covering it up. Now that I faced my fear to find out the truth about his death, I realised I was also facing my pain and walking through it. Feeling my growth within me and the connection to my intuition.

> *Finding out the truth of my dad's death was meeting one of my subconscious fear programs in the eye. I was fearful, it was scary, it was dark, and I felt alone. And it is only by doing that I found the true healing could happen.*

12
PEOPLE PLEASING

After hearing the true details about my dad's death, it seemed like my mind just didn't stop. I didn't want to end up like that, depressed where the only option I felt was for me to end my life. I don't believe I was depressed, but I certainly wasn't happy with my life. I was studying for a degree I'd no interest or love in. Only finishing the course to appease everyone else around me. When I mentioned to friends I wanted to stop studying science and apply for the police force, there was a mixture of responses. They were always along the same line of, "I don't understand why you don't just complete the study first. You only have six months to go?" "Why would you go into policing, that is not the career for you," and, "Police officer? Really? You still want to do that? Why? The career you can get out of the degree you're doing now would be so much better."

To face my fear of learning the truth about my father's death was also the point I came to terms with my mortality. It gave me the motivation to continue with my dream of becoming a police officer. My intuition was telling me to stop studying this degree and apply for the police force. My ego was telling me to complete the science degree. I mean, people expected me to complete it. I didn't want people to think something was wrong with me to not complete the science degree. I didn't want people to think the study was too hard for me. Would I miss the illusion of who my ego wants me to be? I was exhausted by this, it consumed my every being, and I felt like I was on an emotional roller coaster that didn't end. Is this adult life?

My intuition told me one last time to quit my study and apply for the police force. Telling Grant I was quitting the study and applying for the police academy was never an issue. I always had his support in my decisions. It was my mum I was worried about, followed by everyone else.

I asked my mum if she would think any different of me if I quit studying my science degree and applied for the police force. Worried we would have yet another argument, worried she would disapprove and I'd be a disappointment, I blurted it out and was ready to defend myself if she wasn't accepting. But there was no argument, no disapproval, no disappointment, and there was no judgement from her.

Mum said, "Stace, this is your life, and you need to do what you are happy with. If you don't want to complete the degree, you don't have to. If you want to join the police, then go for it. I love you and just want you to be happy."

I quit my science degree and applied for the police force. I received some backlash from friends. And as the years went on, I realised those friends were never really my friends at all. People didn't understand why I quit, didn't understand why I didn't just finish my degree with six months left to go. People didn't understand any of my decisions, people passed judgement on me. I also realised during this time was that they don't need to understand. I realised I didn't need their approval to pursue what I wanted to do, and I didn't need to please anyone but myself. I always wanted to be the good girl. Conditioned into making sure I pleased other people's thoughts and opinions about me.

Being a good girl was the best way I believed, to avoid confrontation, to avoid feeling judged, and to feel accepted. What I didn't realise until I ignored all of that and did what I wanted to do, was that being a people-pleaser was killing me inside. Yes, it was only six months left until I graduated, but again, it was all to please them, not me. I wouldn't use this science degree soon, and if for any reason I needed to study this again, I would most probably start from scratch. Because if I studied this again, it would be because my love and heart was into wanting to learn this information.

However, I haven't desired to study that degree since. The feeling of breaking away from other people's opinions of me, to stop people pleasing, and living the life I wanted to live has been the best decision

I ever made. Submitting the paperwork to cease my study at university was empowering, and I felt so free and much lighter. A weight really did lift off my shoulders.

> *My ego felt confronted when I realised I could not be authentic and people-please at the same time. Pleasing others will never make everyone happy and if you are sacrificing your happiness in the process, is it worth it? This is the question I ask myself, and when I choose my own happiness, focusing on my own evolution, I feel more free within myself.*

PART 2

LEADING TOWARDS MY PURPOSE

13
ARE YOU OKAY?

Whilst I was studying the science degree, a friend told me about a job opportunity that was working as a contractor for the coroner. This meant I would attend various crime scenes around the state and transport the deceased person back to the coroner's office.

It's not your usual job, and people were quick to judge me. I still had my aspirations of becoming a police officer and desire to be a forensic police officer. I thought doing this job would let me see how I was with attending such crime scenes and whether it was the right step to go forward as a forensic police officer. Not only that but doing this job would let me know whether I would be okay with death. I'd been avoiding death for half of my life and there would be no way of hiding from death during this job. I applied and got the job.

The crime scenes would vary from people dying in their sleep, medical episodes resulting in death, car collisions, drownings, suicides, misadventure deaths and suspicious deaths. The ages would range from newborn to the elderly, and would also range from having recently died, to different stages of decomposition and skeletal. I was facing death by not only seeing and picking up body parts including decapitation, and transporting the deceased person, but I was also seeing their families in their most vulnerable state. I not only heard how each person had and/or believed to have died, but I would also see, hear, and feel the energy of their family members'/friends' grief. It also introduced me to other cultures in a new way, especially on how other cultures showed respect to death with ceremonies.

One of my initial concerns before I became a police offer was attending to a deceased who had suicided in similar circumstances to that of my father, and not knowing what my response would be. Especially attending to a deceased where a father died by hanging, in the house or in the yard of where he lived and had a wife and young children. By working for the coroner, that happened many times. I remember on one occasion I attended a suicide of a father. The wife and children were inside as crime scene officers were with the deceased in the garage.

When I turned up, I could tell one police officer waiting out the front near the police car seemed dissociated. He looked quite sad and would not make eye contact. It seemed like his mind was elsewhere as he would often ask me to repeat what I'd said. The person I was working with got frustrated and walked off to find another police officer to get details. Something within me told me to stay, so I did.

I stood next to him with both of our backs leaning on the front of the police car, and both of us looking down the street.

"Are you okay?"

The male officer let out a big sigh before saying, "No. I don't think I am."

"Is there anything I can do for you?"

The male officer said, "I don't think I can go back in there. Back in the garage."

"Can I ask why?"

The male officer said, "Everything about this place reminds me of my uncle right now. The family in the house remind me of my aunty and cousins." He pointed to the garage, referring to the deceased. "And he reminds me of my uncle. He died the same way."

"I am so sorry."

The male officer said, "My uncle died last month. I just need to gather my thoughts, so I have enough strength to go back to the garage after the crime scene officers have finished. My offsider said I need to help place the male in a body bag. I don't want to see his face. It's too much."

"I can deal with the garage. You just take your time here and go into the house when you are ready."

The male officer said, "He hasn't been placed in the body bag yet.

I have to do that. I am the junior officer and my offsider said I have to do it."

"I can do that and sort it out. You just focus on you so you can go in the house with the family."

The male officer said, "Thank you and I'm sorry. I'm never like this at work and I didn't realise this was getting to me."

"There is no need to be sorry. There will be times when jobs are too close to home. That is okay, we are human. Just remember you are not alone and today you did that by talking to me now."

Throughout this whole conversation, I stayed next to this male police officer, but we weren't looking at each other. We were both looking straight ahead.

"Stace," I could hear in the background.

I turned around and saw it was my work partner ushering me to hurry up.

I stood up and turned around to face him. He looked up at me for the first time. I smiled and said, "Now my offsider is calling me. I better go. Take care of yourself," before walking towards the garage.

I want to say it was by pure chance I got this job. But it was my intuition leading me towards my purpose. I spent all my teenage life avoiding death, avoiding talking about death. This moment with the male police officer opened my eyes, I realised I was creating and providing a safe and respectful energy in such a sacred space. To not only the family members but also to the police officers too. It was the starting road towards my purpose.

> *I walked towards the garage ready to face my own fear that day. I knew I was activated when I walked into the garage and yet I felt ready to face the activation. I was nervous about how I may react, but I responded by choosing to continuously breathe whilst holding compassion for myself and those around me.*

14
ATTESTATION DAY

Today is the day. The day I'd been waiting for. It was my attestation parade where I enter as a policing student and leave as a Probationary Constable. It is the graduation ceremony, and all my hard work was coming down to this celebratory day.

This day meant everything to me. This was celebrating my childhood dream, celebrating pushing past people-pleasing to do what I wanted to do, and celebrating the hard work I put in to get to this point.

My family were travelling to the police academy on the morning of my attestation. I would see them out on the parade ground. The day was a gorgeous spring day with a dash of extra heat. And we were wearing our leather jackets for the attestation parade which goes for about two hours. There are always stories of people fainting at these attestation parades and falling flat on their face. The fear was placed inside me. All I kept thinking to myself was:

Red head + leather jacket + heat + standing in the same spot = fainting on my face and breaking my nose.

Thankfully, that disaster didn't happen. I just had an extremely red face, and was sweaty at the end of it all from the heat. However, just before I went out on the parade ground, Grant called me.

"I'm here and with your sisters. I just want to tell you that your mum is not here. I will explain all afterwards, but I don't want you to get upset trying to look for her."

My heart sank. I immediately went to my ego. Why didn't she come?

I thought Mum was accepting of me becoming a police officer. Has she gone back to not accepting my career choice? What was so much more important for her to decide to miss this?

I also felt shame. Shame my mum chose not to attend such an important day in my life. Shame I felt I wasn't worth her time.

I didn't want this to consume me, nor take away from this day I was so happy about. I gave myself a few minutes to acknowledge being angry at Mum for not being there, did some deep breathing, and went out and enjoyed my attestation.

After the attestation I did end up finding out why my mum was not there. Mum was awaiting payment for a large order she had done with her work. Growing up there were many times my mum would not be paid for months at a time with her self-employment as a seamstress. My mum was a hard worker and it would frustrate me how she would have to wait such a long time to receive payment for her work. I was angry and sad mum chose not to attend my attestation, however, I also knew on the other end how much she needed to be paid. Mortgage payments were behind and bills were piling up. I knew if mum was not there to receive her payment it would be quite some time before she would end up receiving it.

At the end of the attestation you throw your hat up in the air in congratulations to yourself and your friends, now colleagues, on all the hard work it took us to get to this point. Standing on that parade ground and giving my oath of office, I had an overall body feeling. It was an intense sense of pride and appreciation within me and it didn't include anyone's validation, just mine. I was living my life the way I wanted it and I had achieved my childhood dream. I became a police officer.

> *There are moments in your life that will be up there with the greatest days of your life. The birth of your children, perhaps even your wedding day. And for me, standing on the parade ground at attestation, throwing my hat up in the air and becoming a police officer was one of the many greatest feelings in my life. It was a moment I will always treasure. When I look back on my attestation day, I remember that feeling. That feeling of achievement and pride within myself. I feel it in my body. It is still one of the best days of my life.*

15
THE FEAR TO SEEK HELP

One – two – three – four – five – six – seven – eight – nine – ten, I am counting out loud as I am performing CPR on an elderly male we just dragged out of a backyard pool. As I am doing these chest compressions, I have one of the elderly male's family members waiting by his head to do the breaths. In the background, I can hear other members of his family crying and a female's voice is screaming, "No this can't be happening."

It was the early hours of the morning while working as a general duties police officer when my offsider and I were called to a house for a missing person. Their father, who was an elderly gentleman with dementia, could not be found. And sadly, my offsider and I found him at the bottom of their green and algae-filled pool.

One – two – three – four – five – six – seven – eight – nine – ten, I am still saying out loud as I was still performing chest compressions and had for several rounds. The ambulance officers turned up and I continued doing chest compressions whilst they were getting their equipment together. One ambulance officer moved the male family member doing breaths out of the way so they could do their thing, whilst I continued with the compressions.

"Just keep going," the ambulance officers said.

I knew the elderly male was deceased already. Not only could I tell by his face, but I just knew within me. I didn't want to believe I was right. I wasn't giving up. In fact, I hoped I would be wrong, and we could bring him back.

One – two – three – four – five – six – seven – eight – nine – ten, I said again as I started another round until, I heard something snap. "Fuck, I think I have just broken one of his ribs," I said to the ambulance officer.

"That's okay, just keep going."

And I did just that, I kept doing the compressions.

A few moments later, the ambulance officers both stopped and one said, "You can stop the compressions now. He's gone."

I stopped, my hands shaking so much I had to place them on my knees. Then I heard the family's screams. Seeing us stopping, they knew their family member had died.

As I walked over to the family, the lady – the elderly gentleman's daughter – started screaming, "Why are you stopping? No, no, no, no."

As she approached me, she went to slightly push me, in a nudge, for me to go back towards her father and keep continuing with compressions. As she went to nudge me, I moved her hands and held them in between mine and said, "I'm sorry. The ambulance officers have confirmed that your dad has died."

The lady fell into my arms in a big hug, crying before her family members went to her where she redirected her hugs to them.

My offsider and I stayed with the family as crime scene officers attended to process the scene before the deceased was taken to the morgue. As I left the house with my offsider and went back to the police station, I knew I wasn't feeling great. It wasn't seeing a person deceased, it was the family and their cries. I felt like I held so much compassion for them during that time, I also forgot to give myself compassion too. There wasn't much debrief back in those days, especially as it wasn't seen as a 'bad deceased or extremely traumatic' to the eyes of others. However, I felt I needed to take some time off to process what happened. But that would mean taking a shift or two off work. That would mean telling work, and then the fear set in. I was a new police officer, still in my probationary period with less than three months service in the job. I was fearful it would damage and delay my chances of finishing my probationary period and future policing opportunities. I was fearful of what other police officers and senior management thought of me, fearful they would believe I wasn't suitable for the job for reaching out. My intuition was telling me to seek help, and I kept resisting because of the fear.

It took three weeks to talk about this job to Grant. I cried in his arms in the middle of the night. I cried over accidentally breaking one of the elderly male's ribs, cried wondering whether I did everything right for them, cried about how I delivered the death message, and cried as I felt I should have done better. That in my head I believed if we'd arrived the house earlier, we could have found him earlier and saved this elderly gentleman. However, the reality of it was this elderly gentleman had been in the water for quite some time. There wasn't a thing I could have done to prevent this man's death, and it was no-one's fault this man died.

> *Years later, I received an intuitive thought to apply to be a Peer Support Officer within the Police Force. Peer Support Officers provide support, guidance, and referrals to police officers who are going through a difficult time whilst on or off duty. Someone to chat and debrief on, someone to be present when in any meetings if needed, and someone to make referrals for other specialist services. But most of all, someone to create and hold space for other police officers when they need it.*

> *When I applied, one thought that came to my head was this incident. I knew I resisted my intuition back then to seek help or even just to talk to another officer. I knew I could make this thought process change for other police officers, and during my time as a Peer Support Officer, I believe I accomplished that.*

16
SHOTS FIRED

Police Radio **Beep. Beep** Possible shots fired at West Avenue, West District.

My offsider for the shift, Senior Constable James Malcolm, and I looked at each other. The look of 'Here we go, this shift just got interesting.' We'd just started our shift and we both ran to the car. Senior Constable Malcolm and I were on the same team and so we worked a lot together.

"West District 14, all cars to meet at the corner of West Avenue and First Street where we vest up," said Sergeant Wright.

"West District 15. Copy, Code Red, two mins," I said.

"West District 16. Copy, Code Red, two mins," said the other car crew working in our command tonight.

We turned up to the meeting point, and we put on our ballistics vests. Sergeant Wright, one of my team leaders, gave us a quick briefing and ended with "Remember, we look out for each other. We are all going home tonight."

And we all nodded in agreement.

Police radio: "Update for all West District cars, possible two fired shots, screaming can be heard, unknown if any injuries."

"West District 14 copy. Myself, 15, and 16 are about to approach the scene. Will advise."

We drove our police vehicle around the corner and parked our cars to approach the house in question. The street was eerily quiet.

I filed in line behind Sergeant Wright, and Senior Constable Malcolm was behind me when we made our way to the front door with our guns drawn and lowered. On the way to the front door, I looked down the driveway and saw what appeared to be a whole garage demolished.

"Can you smell that?" said Sergeant Wright.

"Yea," both Senior Constable Malcolm and I replied.

It smelled like fire and smoke. With pieces spread around in the backyard, it appeared the demolished garage was a recent occurrence.

The front door was open, and we could hear screams and moaning coming from inside. The screams were coming from what sounded like a female. In between her screams I could hear her say, "What do we do?"

The moaning sounded like it was coming from a different person altogether. They sounded like they were in immense pain. As I approached the bottom of the stairs, I had this urge to open and close my fingers from being in a fist to all fingers stretched out. However, I resisted the urge as I still had my firearm drawn and in both of my hands.

Sergeant Wright gave me a nod, and I nodded in return. It was the sign of 'we are ready.' He was to enter the room in one direction, I was to enter in the other, followed by Senior Constable Malcolm.

Sergeant Wright mouthed, "On 3. 1, 2, 3," and in we filed.

As I entered the lounge room, I was gobsmacked by what I saw.

I could see a man sitting on a dining room chair. He was the person I could hear moaning before we entered the house. This man was burnt black from his head until at least his knees, and I remember I could see his white legs as if he was wearing shorts.

There was a female with him, wetting towels and placing it over his body. By the time we came in, there was a towel over both of his hands and she was wetting another towel whilst saying to the male, "Everything will be okay."

When the female saw us run into the room, she let out a huge cry. It was a cry of relief she wasn't there alone. "Please help me."

I holstered my firearm and again had the urge to open and close my hands from a fist to having all my fingers out. As I approached the man, I saw his face and body had open wounds pouring with blood. The smell of his burnt skin was overpowering. Not only was this man in intense pain and could not move, but he was having trouble breathing. My attention went straight to the man's hands. Covered with towels, I could see blood was soaking through them, and fast.

"What was he holding when the explosion happened?" I asked.

The man moaning was nodding his head in a yes motion and the female, who was his wife, said, "He was making and packing home bullets. Filling the cases with gun powder with home grown ammunition in the garage when it somehow sparked causing the explosion."

"How many fingers?" I asked.

"Eight, including both of his thumbs," said the wife.

Sergeant Wright, Senior Constable Malcolm, and the other car crew were all helping give first aid to the male.

"Do you have the fingers?" I asked her.

"No, I don't," she cried.

I had an intense feeling within me. I felt like I would find the fingers and I knew the possibility of having this man's fingers reattached would be high if I could find them and have them put on ice as soon as possible. "I'll find the fingers in hopes they can be reattached," I said before running out the door.

"It's like a needle in a haystack out there," Sergeant Wright yelled back but I didn't stop to respond.

I ran to the site of where the garage used to be and stood in front of all the rubble. There was only one wall frame standing. Everything was in pieces on the ground like someone tipped 1000 puzzle pieces out of the box on the floor in a pile. There appeared to be no active fires, but it smelled so much of smoke and powder residue. Sergeant Wright was right. As I stood at the start of the demolition site, it felt like I was looking for needles in a haystack.

I closed my eyes, took a deep breath, coughed because I forgot about the full-on smoke smell I was facing, put on my gloves and walked onto the garage demolition site. Trying to find stable ground in between wood and half burnt plaster, I approached a spot within the garage demolition site that drew my energy the most. I pulled back a piece of half burnt plaster and I found a finger. I picked it up, put the finger in my left hand, turned around and found another finger poking out from under a piece of wood. Before I knew it, I was picking up fingers left, right and centre. I picked up six fingers in total.

I had my hands together carrying the bunch of fingers and ran inside the house. As I ran inside the door I yelled, "I need plastic bags and ice." At the same time, ambulance officers were leaving with the male in the back of the ambulance with lights and sirens.

Rushing to the kitchen, I placed the fingers on the kitchen bench and saw there were plastic bags near me.

Perfect.

I took two bags and tipped their contents – cans and soft drink bottles – onto the bench. I got one plastic bag and placed all the fingers inside it. Someone gave me trays of ice cubes and I placed the ice cubes in another bag. I then placed the bag with the fingers inside the bag with the ice cubes.

Sergeant Wright said, "We told the ambos you found fingers. We will sort everything out here and try and find the last two fingers. Just drive those to the hospital in hopes they can reattach his fingers."

"How is he?" I asked.

"Critical. Most of his body is burnt and not sure what damage has been sustained inside," replied Sergeant Wright.

"I'll make my way over," I said and ran to the car whilst carrying the fingers with ice.

I got into the police car and thought, 'Where do I put them?' I didn't want to place them anywhere for it to move, have the ice fall out or the fingers fall out. Because we had our ballistic vests out to wear to attend this job, we had our personal police bags not only thrown around in the back seat but the front seat as well. Everywhere seemed full of stuff.

I took off my ballistic vest and threw it in the back seat. I placed the plastic bag in my lap, between my legs, put the lights and sirens on and started the drive. "West District 15 alpha urgent," I said to police radio.

"West District 15 go ahead," said police radio.

"West District 15 alpha, I am proceeding Code Red to West District Hospital with six fingers on board. Please advise emergency I will arrive in five to ten minutes."

"West District 15, copy," said police radio.

Acting on your non-local intuition is a reminder that everything is energy.

17
WE FOUND THE OTHER TWO

I got to the hospital, handed over the bag of fingers, and made my way back to the crime scene driving under lights and sirens.

Me to police radio: "West District 15 alpha, I have left the hospital and returning to the crime scene in hopes to find the remaining two fingers. Please advise if they have already been found?"

Police Radio: "West District 14 go ahead"

Sergeant Wright: "West District 14, no, we haven't. We are still looking."

Me: "West District 15 alpha, understood. Code Red, five minutes."

When I returned, Sergeant Wright and Senior Constable Malcolm were still looking the other two fingers. "How the hell did you find the other fingers, Stace? It is chaos here," said Sergeant Wright.

"I don't know. I just knew where to go," I said. And that was the truth. I just knew where to go and looked. I stood in the area where I found the six fingers and I knew the remaining two fingers were not in this area. It was a knowing within me followed by a feeling. I took four steps away from where I was, pulled up some wood and plaster, and there they were. The remaining two fingers. "Got them," I yelled.

I ran back inside and got more plastic bags.

"There is no more ice. It was used for when you took the first lot of my husband's fingers," his wife said.

I looked at her and I felt the immense pain she had in her heart. She was trying to get things together to go to the hospital. She wasn't allowed in the ambulance as they had so many ambulance officers in the ambulance helping her husband.

I held her hand and said, "I am sorry you are experiencing this. I am doing everything I can for your husband. Is there anything I can do for you?"

The lady hugged me so tight and whispered, "You are doing it already."

I felt her warmth through her hug and knew it was because I gave her compassion and a sacred space to let her know whatever she was feeling was okay.

I grabbed some frozen vegetables, shoved bags of them in the plastic bag, followed by the two remaining fingers in another bag. The same as before, I placed the bag of fingers in the bag of frozen vegetables, tied off the top, and yelled out, "Sarge, I'm going back to the hospital," as I ran to the car.

"West District 15 alpha. I am back on my way to the hospital to this job with the remaining two fingers. Code Red, five minutes, please alert the hospital of my arrival," I said to the police radio.

"Copy West District 15," replied police radio.

I dropped off the remaining two fingers to the nurses waiting for me at emergency. After having two separate times of holding a bag of fingers on ice on my legs, it was safe to say, the water soaked my pants. Now it looked like I'd wet myself. So off I went to the bathroom in the hospital, using the hand dryer on my pants. I focused on my breath as I dried myself, feeling myself calm down, self-regulating my nervous system before I headed back to the house, which was declared a crime scene.

> *As the years past, there were several times I would be at a job where I would need to pick up fingers, package them with ice and convey them to hospital in hopes they could be reattached. I was able to show resilience each time. Showing flexibility in the challenges I faced and the flexibility in the way I was able to respond emotionally to stress. I could only ensure I had resilience by acknowledging and working on my nervous system.*

18
NEIGHBOURHOOD DISPUTE

If you thought driving fingers back and forth from a hospital would be enough for one shift, think again, because this is me. I am my own shining star.

At 5:30 am, after locating fingers from the 'bomb job', Senior Constable Malcolm and I were at the police station. We were exhausted after doing all the other jobs within the command whilst the other car crew did the 'explosion job.' And there came another job.

Police radio: "West District cars, you have one job outstanding being a noise complaint."

I felt the need to attend to this job. A knowing within myself.

Me: "Malcolm, we need to go to this job."

Senior Constable Malcolm: "Nah, it's just a noise complaint. Day shift can chase it up. We have been smashed this shift."

Me: "I know we have, but I know we need to go to this job. I will do the job, I promise."

Senior Constable Malcolm reluctantly agreed, and we drove to the noise complaint.

"You're too eager to work, Stace," he mumbled on the way.

I spoke to the person who made the call to police. The man said he was angry at their neighbour who started their car and left it running in the driveway for the last thirty minutes.

"Do you get along with your neighbours?"

He said, "Yea. It's an older couple. They keep to themselves."

"Does this normally happen where their car is running in their driveway?"

"No, but that's not the point. Go over there and have that car turned off."

I could see Senior Constable Malcolm, who was standing in my peripheral vision, moving forward to approach this man. I signalled Senior Constable Malcolm to stay where he was.

"I will go next door. Have a great day." I walked away.

Senior Constable Malcolm walked up next to me and said, "I can't believe you didn't go off at him for how he was speaking to you."

"There is no need. His morning won't get any quieter, anyway."

Senior Constable Malcolm said, "What do you mean?"

"Something is not right. Maybe we should get the first aid kit from the car before we walk in?"

Senior Constable Malcolm said, "Stace, don't be silly. We don't need that."

We walked past the car that was running in the driveway, up to the front door. The screen door was shut. However, the front door was open. As I went to open the front door an elderly gentleman burst out into the front yard from the front screen door. Then he turned around and ran back inside the house. He was clenching his chest and was gasping for air.

I ran inside the house and his wife was standing in the lounge room.

"He's having a heart attack," she screamed, filled with panic.

I said to Senior Constable Malcolm, "Get the first aid kit," before I got my police radio and said, "West District 15, urgent."

Police Radio: "West District 15 only, go ahead."

Me: "West District 15, I need an ambulance to our location. I have a male in his 80s who is appearing to have a heart attack. Conscious, and having extreme trouble breathing."

Police Radio: "Copy West District 15."

Sergeant Wright: "West District 14, Code Red, five minutes."

I turned to the elderly man and said, "Sir, can you—" and that's when I saw it. I saw the fearful look in the elderly man's eyes. The fear of the pain he was experiencing, the fear of not breathing, the fear of dying. And I knew and felt within my body he wasn't just asking, "Help me." He was asking, "Don't let me die."

I saw this in the microsecond before he fell to the ground like a tonne of bricks.

Senior Constable Malcolm came in with the first aid kit and lateral mask as the elderly man fell to the ground. It felt like Senior Constable Malcolm was gone for ages but he was gone for less than a minute.

Senior Constable Malcolm and I turned the man over and his face was blue. His jaw was locked. I checked for a pulse and there wasn't one.

Me: "West District 15 Urgent, patient unresponsive, commencing CPR."

I commenced compressions to his chest whilst Senior Constable Malcolm used the lateral mask for breathing.

As I was doing the chest compressions, I could hear his wife howling and screaming, "Don't let him die."

She said it multiple times in a high pitch scream filled with fear. I had to block out her screams. I focused on the chest compressions, watching for any reaction to the elderly man in hopes he showed positive signs of breathing. Sergeant Wright turned up as Senior Constable Malcolm and I were performing CPR. He was speechless. I remember our eyes locked as I was doing the compressions. We were not seeing any progress, and this was before the days of having a defibrillator in the police vehicles. The ambulance had not turned up, and I could see the panicked thought in Sergeant Wright's eyes of, "I hope he doesn't die." I had the same thought myself.

As I was doing the chest compressions, I knew he was still present in his body. He hadn't died, and he wouldn't die in this moment. In what felt like forever doing chest compressions, with still no ambulance showing at this time, we got a sign. The elderly man gasped for air and his eyes opened like he'd been jolted with life.

Ambulance officers turned up and Senior Constable Malcolm and I moved out of the way so they could tend to him. His wife ran up to me and gave me the tightest hug. She didn't need to say anything as I could feel it all within the hug that she wanted to say thank you. We then got the car keys to turn off their car ignition, still running in the driveway.

Once the ambulance left to take the elderly man and his wife to the hospital, Sergeant Wright, Senior Constable Malcolm and I left the house. In the front yard we all looked at each other with a sigh of relief.

"I thought this shift was busy enough with a bomb exploding in someone's face but adding on this at the end really takes the cake," Sergeant Wright said.

Back at the police station Senior Constable Malcolm asked, "How did you know that guy was going to have a heart attack, Stace?"

"I didn't," I answered.

"But you even asked for the first aid bag before we even got to the front door," asked Senior Constable Malcolm.

"I can't explain it," I said. "But when the job came over, I just knew within myself that I needed to be there. I wasn't sure why or what was going to happen. When the neighbour was going on about his reason for his noise complaint, I then got another feeling that we would need the first aid kit. Although I wasn't sure why or what was going to happen."

"Well, whatever you can do, it's working, Stace. You found eight fingers none of us could find and did CPR to save a man's life all in one shift," said Senior Constable Malcolm.

It is amazing what events police remember throughout their careers. As I was writing this book, I spoke to Sergeant Wright and Senior Constable Malcolm about this shift with these two jobs. Sergeant Wright could not remember that specific shift at all, yet Senior Constable Malcolm remembered every detail.

19
CHRISTMAS ANGEL

A few days later, I was working a night shift on Christmas Eve. I swapped with someone else so they could spend it with their kids.

"Stace, someone to see you at the front counter," the station constable said.

I walked to the front counter and saw the wife of the elderly male Senior Constable Malcolm and I performed CPR on a few shifts before. She was standing in the front foyer, with her best Sunday clothes on, wearing a matching hat and carried a small handbag.

"Hello," I said. "How is your husband?"

"He is good. He is home now from the hospital. He did have a heart attack but thankfully he is on medication and should be okay," she replied.

"And how are you?"

The lady looked like she was about to cry. Her lip started quivering and her hand started shaking. I walked closer to her and held out my hand. The lady placed her hand on mine, and I placed my other hand on top of hers. "How are you?" I asked again.

"I'm doing well. Everything has been so busy with what happened I haven't had a chance to stop," she replied.

I said, "You have done an amazing job being there for your husband. Remember you need to look after yourself too," I replied.

"I came to say thank you. If you were not there that day, I don't think my husband would be alive. You, my dear, are a Christmas angel," she said.

I could see the elderly lady was on the edge and about to cry. I gave her a hug.

"It's okay if you want to cry. You have been through a lot these last few days."

The lady cried in my arms. I didn't say anything and just held her as she cried. When she finished, she got herself a handkerchief from her handbag and wiped her eyes.

"Thank you," she said. "I needed a good cry to let it out."

For me, being a police officer was about helping people. This event emphasised that the work a police officer does has ripples effects in so many lives. I knew it, but didn't see and feel it until this moment.

20
BECOMING A DETECTIVE

Whilst working as a uniformed police officer in General Duties, I would often be the first car on the scene for serious crime jobs. It would be me and whoever I was working with that day, and instead of turning left to continue a patrol, I would turn right. Just because I felt it, a knowing I should do it. It was my intuition, and I was letting it guide me. To only be followed moments later with a call from Police Radio on an urgent job and lo-and-behold, I would either be on the actual street where it happened or close to it.

Being the first police officer on scene at a job and performing my duties meant, depending on the job, detectives would always see my work. Sometimes detectives would assist me with the job, providing me guidance, and other times – especially with serious jobs – they would have to take carriage of the job. Meaning they would become the officer in charge and investigate instead of me. Half the time, as they would be recalled to duty to attend the job, by the time they came to the station I would be already working on their paperwork – such as crime scene warrants. Which saved them a lot of time too.

One day, I was doing paperwork in the police station when the Investigations Manager at the time, Detective Senior Sergeant Hart, came up to me and said, "Stacey, when are you putting in for your A-list?"

Doing your A-list is the starting point in working in the detective's office.

"I thought you need to work in uniform for three years before you can transfer anywhere," I said.

"Not all the time," he replied. "You should put one (report) in. You have a keen eye for criminal investigation and would make a great detective."

To be honest, I'd never thought of working in the detectives at that point. I was so focused on working in forensics with the cops prior to joining the police force. Whilst working as a police officer, I reflected on the possibility of becoming a forensics police officer and came to the realisation I didn't want to do that anymore. I wanted to do something else. But work as a detective? Should I? The answer I received from within myself was "Yes."

Where would this lead me? I wasn't sure. I didn't have to understand it, I just had to follow the breadcrumbs my intuition was telling me. I put in my application and after eighteen months working in uniform, I commenced my career in the detective's office.

To be a female in what is dominantly a patriarchal-run career, I was grateful to have leaders such as Detective Sergeant Hart. A leader is not about the rank of a person. It's what they embody and give out to the world.

21
CAN I ASK YOU A QUESTION?

The time had come where after finishing my last few shifts in General Duties, I would be going into the detective's office and working out of there. On my last shift before going into the Detectives, my partner and I were called to a missing person found deceased located in bushland. When my partner and I got there, we found a male lying face-down on the ground. We found a knife next to him and could see several deep cuts to his wrists consistent with self-inflicted wounds.

There wasn't anything suspicious on this death. The male was in his mid-50s, had a spouse and children, and was battling with his mental health. He was reported missing as he'd left a note saying he was ending his life. By all accounts I was looking at a suicide. As we were waiting for crime scene officers to attend, the detectives turned up.

The senior detective got all the details, looked around and said, "Well, Stace, there is nothing suspicious about this death. Looks like this one is yours."

"No worries," I replied. "But when crime scene officers arrive and turn him over to see the stab wound to his heart, I will call you back."

I said it not realising at first I'd spoken. I took a step back and wondered why I said that? And why did I say this out loud? I was meant to be working in the detective's office starting my next shift, and this detective must think I am an idiot now.

The detectives laughed at me before leaving, and I felt like I'd just embarrassed myself. Crime scene officers arrived, and they did their work.

"Stace," one crime scene officer said. "Come here and take a look at this."

I walked over and saw that crime scene have turned over the deceased male. And there to his heart area were multiple stab wounds to the chest. On closer inspection, they didn't appear to be deep wounds, and still appeared self-inflicted, but none the less, they were stab wounds. I was in complete shock. I called back to the Senior detective.

"Hey, it's Stace. Um, you will not believe me. But crime scene officers have turned over this male and no joke, he has stab wounds to his heart area."

They came out right away. It still appeared to be a suicide, however, the detectives were talking about taking the job instead. I had the intuitive hit within me to keep this job. Rethinking my decision on wanting to keep the job, I thought it was a good idea as it would be a coronial brief anyway. I approached the senior detective and said, "I know you are wondering whether you should take the job," followed with a cheeky smirk. "And I do remember you saying you would do this job if he had stab wounds to his chest. But since I am going to the detectives next week, can I just keep this job and work on it whilst in the detective's office?"

Of course, the senior detective would be happy, and he said, "Yes" straight away.

This would be a part of the coronial investigation that I was to put before the coroner. I'd organised for his wife, Rebecca, to attend the police station over the next coming days. Rebecca and I spent quite some time together obtaining her statement. That is always the way when taking a statement from a close family member. When we finished the statement Rebecca said, "Can I ask you a question?"

"Sure."

"My children, who are all older and in their 20s and 30s, don't know all their father's details on how he chose to die. They don't know about how he stabbed himself in the heart before he cut his wrists. They just know he died by suicide, but they don't know how at this point. Would I be a bad person if I didn't tell them how he killed himself? Would I be a bad person if I never told them this information?"

I knew this question wasn't just for her but another layer for me and my healing. Although the details of my father's death and this man's were different, the underlying theme was: not telling their children details about their deaths. I believed at this stage I was in a healed state towards my mum not telling the truth of my father's death straight away. And so, I knew this was about my mum and seeing her perceptions more in depth.

"What are your reasons for not wanting to tell them?" I asked.

"I am scared they will be upset and have mental health issues arise from it," she responded.

"You have just gone through something traumatic with your husband choosing to end his life the way he did. I can understand why you are wanting to withhold information from them, and I can understand their thoughts on wanting to ask questions, be curious, and want to know details on how one of their parents has died," I said.

"I'm just so confused. I don't know what to do. I don't want my children hating me if they found out later," Rebecca said.

I replied, "Being scared is normal. Being in fear to tell your children something that you know is going to be upsetting to them is normal. Worried about what may happen after knowing this information is normal. This is the time you need your children, and your children need you. For you all to grieve together. For you all to be there for each other. For the love to continue in this family over the fear."

Rebecca nodded in agreement.

I said, "Can you answer this question? If your children were to find out the truth down the track, would it mean they would be grieving again?"

Rebecca paused and took in that question for quite some time before answering, "Good question."

I gave Rebecca details on grief counselling for herself, and her adult children to do separately or together as a family and she left the police station.

> *After Rebecca left, I sat at my desk in the statement room and just breathed. I had so many thoughts going on in my head. Did I say the right things or was I influenced and biased from my personal experience? Or was it because of my personal experience, I was the best person for this matter? However, once the chatter in my mind quietened, I knew deep within my heart I was placed in her life to be a messenger.*

22
ANGEL

This story of a gorgeous little girl, Angel, and her death is a story that will always be with me throughout my policing career and beyond. When I was writing this book, Angel's energy would pop into my head. I knew it was my intuition telling me to talk about her and how it formed a part of the breadcrumbs that lead me to how I work as a detective. I originally didn't want to mention this story, however, this story was a defining moment for me not only in my career but my personal life. I kept dismissing it, mainly because the story of Angel was traumatic for me. It has taken me almost ten years to process and talk about Angel to this degree. And so, with that being said, please know the next chapter can be traumatic or activating for some. If you don't wish to read it, skip this chapter.

If you choose to read, please read with caution.

Working as a Contractor for the coroner before I was a police officer, and being a police officer for several years, I have seen death. I felt like I'd seen every type of death possible and every crime scene possible. This also included an unfortunate number of children's deaths as well. Angel's death was something different to me.

I'd been working as a detective for a while and was getting busy with some big investigations with some smaller ones in-between. On one morning, I woke up to get ready for work and I remember saying to Grant how uneasy I felt for work that day. A feeling within my chest that would not go away, a feeling of 'don't bother planning anything after work.' I assumed a job would come in and I would do overtime and left it at that.

The day at work started well. But the uneasy feeling was still there because the shift wasn't over yet.

Police radio: *Beep. Beep* "West District cars to South West side. Male has arrived home to find his sister and niece deceased in the kitchen, possible homicide."

As soon as I heard it, I knew this wasn't all of it. I knew there was more, but I didn't know what.

I got into the car with my offsider, who I was working with that shift, and we made our way there. As we got to the house, I saw a neighbour was out the front. He pointed to inside the house and said, "The boy is still in there."

The boy the neighbour was referring to was the boy who contacted police. The boy who found his sister and niece deceased in their kitchen when he came home from school.

I ran inside and saw two of our uniformed police who got there before us, and a teenage boy standing on one side of the island kitchen bench. The teenage boy was crying hysterically, telling the uniform officers the female was his sister called Abigail and the child was his niece, Abigail's daughter, Angel. I asked them if they could continue their conversation in the backyard for the moment. I wanted everyone out of the house for a couple of reasons. One, I didn't want that young man to keep looking at what was on the other side of the kitchen bench and two, it was now a crime scene.

I looked over the kitchen bench and I saw a vision I will never forget. Abigail was lying on the kitchen floor. There were large puncture wounds all the way up her arms and legs followed by puncture wounds to her chest. A large kitchen knife was next to her hand. There was blood all over her chest area that spilled over her body onto the kitchen floor.

Beside her was her three-year-old daughter, Angel, and she was also deceased. Angel had what appeared to be wounds to her chest as blood covered her chest area too. What became the shock I wasn't expecting was Angel's head. Decapitated from her body, it lay within a hand width away from her neck. Blood that started from the neck had surrounded the outline of her head.

It took everything within me not to go over to Angel and close her eyes. It was clear Angel was dead, and I didn't want to disturb the crime scene. Although it appeared this was a murder/suicide, this still required a thorough and proper investigation without me interfering with a crime scene. Before I left the house, I looked over at Angel's face. Even though I knew she was dead and there was nothing I could do to save her, I could not help but look at her again.

> *There will be certain jobs within your career as a police officer that stay with you forever. This job for me is one of them.*

23
DEATH MESSAGE

As I walked out the front of the house, I was told Abigail's mum and Angel's grandmother, Sarah, was due to arrive home any minute. I saw a car pull up and a lady get out. I could tell who she was before she confirmed it. Sarah had the same beautiful face as Abigail and Angel. As Sarah got out of the car, I saw the panic in her eyes, the panic whilst she looked around at all the police cars there by that point.

I saw her pace pick up from a walk to a slow run, and as she got to the driveway, I ran to her whilst signalling to the uniform police officers approaching us to stay back. I knew she knew something was wrong. And I knew I would have to break the bad news to her. Sarah held my upper arms as I held hers. I was holding her back, so she didn't pass me as she was trying to get around me.

"Sarah—" I said. Sarah interrupted me.

"No, no, no, please don't tell me my daughter is dead." She screamed.

I said, "Sarah, can you please follow me to the seats next door to your house?"

"I am not going anywhere. Please don't tell me my daughter is dead."

I could feel her fingers tightening around my arms. Her body was trying to help her prepare for the news I was about to deliver. I looked into her eyes, and I could tell her eyes were pleading with me, pleading to not confirm what she asked was correct. I knew I had to tell her. Sarah was facing her fear of knowing her life would change forever. Sarah knew this and still wanted to walk through the front door.

"I'm so sorry to tell you that Abigail is dead."

Sarah clung close to me, nestling in my shoulder as she howled. Abigail had post-natal depression where the family and her daughter herself tried to get mental health assistance. And sadly today, Sarah faced the reality her daughter took her own life.

"What about my granddaughter, Angel?"

This was the part I was fearing, knowing the words I said would change her life again the way I'd done not even a minute earlier. I took a deep breath, looked into her eyes and said, "I'm sorry Sarah, but Angel is dead as well."

Sarah howled even louder, screaming.

"NO, NO, NO."

She urinated in her pants from the complete shock. I kept holding her as we both slunk down to the ground of the driveway together. I sat next to her and hugged her as she cried into my shoulder. I didn't say anything. After delivering those two death messages, I knew my role was to not talk and just hold space for her that she needed during this time. I don't know how long I was holding her in her driveway for, but it didn't bother me. I knew my job was to give her the sacred space she needed. I didn't tell her everything will be okay, because it wasn't okay. I didn't tell her to hurry up. Instead, I allowed her the time she needed. I didn't care what people may have thought, because their opinions meant nothing to me.

I could see other police, both uniform and plain clothes were looking and feeling uncomfortable. I could feel them slinking away and feeling grateful they were not in my position of delivering the news. Other police would, from time to time, try to approach. I knew it was for me to move her along from the driveway. I gave them the hand wave to say, "Go away."

When Sarah was ready, we moved from the driveway. I organised underwear and clothes for her, and a neighbour offered for Sarah to use their shower. Whilst I was arranging this for her, another detective asked Sarah if she would provide a statement to police as investigations into Abigail's and Angel's death were commencing. Sarah said she would make the statement to me only.

I drove Sarah to the police station so I could take her statement. Here I am in a car by myself with Sarah. I had just delivered her two painful and life changing pieces of news. I didn't know what to say on the drive.

Sarah: "You're taking my statement, aren't you?"

Me: "Yes, I am, Sarah."

Sarah: "Good, because right now I don't want to make a statement to anyone else but you."

Me: "Why is that?"

Sarah: "Because I know from you there is no judgement. I urinated my pants, and you still sat and hugged me. You were there for me. And most of all, you haven't judged Abigail for what she did to Angel before she killed herself."

Sarah's phone rang before I could respond. It was Sarah's husband. He was overseas helping his mother. Sarah asked if I could help her tell her husband Abigail and Angel were dead. I agreed and pulled over the car. As Sarah answered and put the phone call on loudspeaker, she started crying as she tried telling her husband what happened.

"No, it's not true. Please say this is not true, Sarah. Please!" her husband pleaded in between his screams.

Sarah froze. I took the phone from her and held her hand.

"Hi, my name is Stacey, and I am one of the detectives attached to West District. Is this Sarah's husband?"

"Yes. I am overseas now and called as soon as I could. Please say it is not true. Please say Abigail and Angel are not dead?" he replied.

"I'm deeply sorry to say that it is true. Abigail and Angel both died today."

I could hear Sarah's husband wailing through the phone. I could feel his pain in his heart from hearing this news. And so, I just continued creating the space Sarah and her husband needed in the car.

Sarah's husband booked the next flight back to Australia before I reached the police station.

> *It is never easy having to give a death message. No matter if you have time to practice in your head beforehand or not, you know you are saying something that will change their lives forever. You know they will remember this moment. You know you're taking away any hope they may have for their loved one to still have a chance for survival. And it is at these times, whilst you hold compassion for them, you hold compassion for yourself to give the news.*

24
CREATING AND HOLDING SPACE

It seems insensitive, does it not? A woman has just been told her daughter and granddaughter are dead, and here we are trying to get a statement from her. The same as her son coming home to find his sister and niece dead in the kitchen, and here we are trying to get a statement from them. Yes, what happened was a murder/suicide, and this investigation required the same devoted attention to the investigation as if it were two murders. We needed to get information from people and that's done through obtaining their statements.

I then spent the next six hours obtaining Sarah's statement. During that time, not only was I obtaining information I needed for the investigation but when Sarah felt she needed to cry at certain parts of the statement, we stopped, and she cried. When things felt overwhelming or the feeling would approach, I would coach Sarah through some breathing exercises. When Sarah closed her eyes, her face showing great pain as she was recalling some events, I held her hand and lightly tapped it. And when Sarah just felt the need to growl or yell, I would sit aside to let her release any type of sounds she needed.

Sarah and her husband knew Abigail used a knife, which included stabbing Angel before using it on herself. But no one mentioned the decapitation part initially. I also went to the city morgue to be present for Abigail's and Angel's post-mortems. The officer in charge and supervisors organised a counsellor from the city morgue to accompany them, so they had further support and made arrangements when the news was given.

After this job, I sought professional help through the Employee Assistance Program, which is a program police officers can access to obtain professional help in various areas. For me, it was speaking to a psychologist, and I did for a few months. I felt guilty for how I told Sarah about her daughter and granddaughter's death. I felt like I didn't do enough for Sarah, and even though I could not have prevented this from happening, I still felt guilty knowing when Angel was being murdered, I wasn't there to prevent it from happening. But the progress of the sessions frustrated me. The psychologist fixated on the fact I went to both Abigail and Angel's post-mortems. I felt like my thoughts about Abigail and Angel weren't being listened to, as I had spoken about before. Instead of seeing someone else, I just stopped going altogether.

What I didn't realise until years after this job, upon reflection, was taking this statement from Sarah was the first time I felt I really created and held a sacred space for the person I was obtaining the statement for. One of the reasons I am here on this earth, a defining moment. Having this soul experience in this body now, is to create and hold a sacred space for people, with no judgement, in all of their vulnerability, so they can speak and let out any emotion and sound they feel is needed for that moment. And since obtaining Sarah's statement, I have been creating and holding a sacred space for people in not only my work as a police officer, but also beyond that, ever since.

It took me years to be able to even speak of Angel and this job. Everything surrounding this event felt overwhelming for me. Throughout my own trauma healing journey, I realised I was avoiding anything related to this job out of fear. As I allowed the fear to slowly be present and surrounded it with love, the fear behind it released. Releasing that fear ultimately allowed me to transmute the fear into love. It allowed me to not be stuck by it and to not allow the fear to be the leader of my life.

25
GET OUT OF HERE

After five years of working as a police officer, and three-and-a-half years of that in criminal investigation, I was at a point in my life where I needed a change and to step out of my comfort zone. I knew I still wanted to work in criminal investigation, and it was just my time at that police station was complete.

What was stopping me? Fear. So much fear smooshed in together to create one big ball of fear. The fear of going somewhere new and starting fresh again. Working at the same place made me feel comfortable in what can be an unpredictable occupation. Then there was the fear of making a mistake, being blamed for mistakes, not being forgiven for my mistakes, and being criticised for any mistakes made. Another fear of stopping me was people stereotyping/judging me. I was twenty-six years old, and a designated detective within the police force. Not only that, but I had a baby face and looked younger than my age. Don't believe me? I once turned up to a high school to speak to a student and the administration lady yelled at me saying I should have been in the main hall with all the other Year 12 students. I should be flattered, but I was out wanting to show I could do all the jobs. But I knew within myself I needed to move on. I needed to push past the unknown. I knew there was so much more out there for me to learn, and I needed to move on to learn whatever it was.

Denying this feeling left me feeling overwhelmed and resentful. The alchemy of the office had changed. It wasn't a bad thing. It is just a part of the cyclical nature of an office. Adding to that, I'd changed too. I was at a point where everything within my office was irritating me, and I was feeling suffocated. I was in a relationship with Grant and had no children at that stage. I was a hard worker, determined, motivated, a dutiful soldier and a good girl. I was following the old patriarchal ways of trying to make a career in a man's world. Always pushing myself, always striving for more, and always saying yes. I never created my own boundaries, which, as a result, neglected my own needs and made me lose a bit of myself in the process. I felt my boundaries were not worthy and important. That I should be grateful I rose through to the detectives quickly and so I felt I should just suck it up and get on with it. Every time I placed a boundary, it was my intuition giving me the opportunity to get this side of me in place. Looking back, I can see the signs, but at the time, I disregarded and tried to block receiving and listening to my intuition. I chose fear of speaking up instead of boundaries, and when I recognised I was doing that, I felt it was too late.

However, it was never too late. My intuition again was trying to communicate with me. I failed to act on my intuition because of fear. Fear of being judged, fear of not being perceived as the good girl and fear I may not get their validation I was a hard and good worker. I was again people pleasing and on another emotional roller coaster.

I wanted to get out of my office. I wanted to transfer to another detective's office, but my fear of transferring took over and my over thinking was sky-high:

- What if I transfer and it is the same office dynamics as this, where it is filled with patriarchal ideas on how to run an office?
- And transferring means I would be in tenure again and must be there for at least three years. What if I hate my new office, and I am stuck there for three years?
- I wanted children at some point. What if the next office isn't flexible with part-time workers? The fear of starting fresh elsewhere is strong too.
- I have such a natural resting bitch face everyone will think I'm just a bitch and no-one will talk to me.
- How will I make friends?

The reality was, I was feeling overworked, burnt out and emotionally exhausted. I kept thinking "things will get better" which was merely an excuse to avoiding my intuition. The fear was just too strong for me. I let the fear in.

26

EMOTIONAL ROLLERCOASTER

I felt like I could not talk to anyone about being on this emotional roller coaster at the time I wanted to transfer. I felt the responses I would receive were, "You should be grateful. Other people would love to be in your position."

I was grateful, but I also knew I got to where I was because of my hard work. I could not make sense of it in my head. I didn't reach out to anyone. Besides work friends, I didn't know who else I could talk to that would understand what I was going through and keep my thoughts discreet. There are Peer Support Officers and the Employee Assistance Program within the police, however, at the time I felt ashamed to use their services. I felt like my problems were small compared to what others might need those services for. I dismissed me, which left me feeling lost and highly stressed about going to work each day.

I started driving to work and hoping a car would hit me on the way so I didn't have to go to work and do my shift. This went on for a few months before one day on the way to work I was again hoping it would happen. Something inside me told me to pull over, this has been going on long enough. I pulled over two streets before my station and it hit me. I'd been in this state before. I'd hoped a car would hit me to help me decide to leave studying my science degree, and I was doing it again. I was hoping something outside of me would help decide what I already knew I needed.

I then felt a wave of relief come over me. I was relieved that I understood what my intuition was telling me, in a way that meant I would hopefully recieve the information. I realised it was time for me to face my fear and find a way to transfer. I needed to get out of there. Stepping out of my comfort zone, and overcoming the fear of starting fresh in a new place, wasn't necessarily a bad thing. I knew it was a good move to make. And as that wave of relief set over me, I just cried. I let those tears out, whilst parked on the side of the road. I moved that stagnant energy. I was now listening.

On my next shift, I went into work, sat at my desk, took a deep breath, and thought, "Who can I contact to see if there are vacancies at another police command?" And the answer arrived within me instantly. "Detective Senior Sergeant Hart."

Detective Senior Sergeant Hart had been transferred out of our command for a good three to four years by that point. What harm could an email do? And so, I emailed him asking if he had any vacancies, and if there wasn't any, could he let me know when they would have one?

Within an hour, I received a reply. Yes, he remembered me, and yes, he would love to have me work in his office. They didn't have any vacancies and he stated he would let me know when they did. At the end of the email was a final paragraph. That earlier this morning he'd sent an email on a vacancy within the North District. I didn't receive this email as I was in a different region. But nonetheless, Detective Senior Sergeant Hart forwarded me the job vacancy in case I was interested.

I read the job vacancy, and I intuitively knew this job was mine. The feeling wasn't me being overconfident. I felt it within my heart that if I applied for this job, this job would be mine and I would learn big and great lessons working there. I applied for the job and the position was mine. Yes! The weight was lifted. I didn't feel trapped and stale.

Without having loyalty to yourself means you are abandoning yourself. The unsettling feeling within me knew I was meant for more, and giving in to my fear meant I wasn't being loyal to myself. It took me a long time, but I did eventually realise we are meant to grow and evolve and that may include moving on from certain places of work to allow that to happen.

Years later, I felt the urge to get out of my comfort zone again. To be challenged and learn more. I followed my intuition and worked in a different unit. This time, I did not listen to my fears and ego of going somewhere new. They were never given a thought. I intuitively knew I needed to make the steps out of my comfort zone to work in another unit. And it was because I listened and took those small steps forward that I had no desire for myself to be involved in a car accident. I was listening and acting on my intuition. I was evolving and growing with each layer.

PART 3
SEEDS ARE PLANTED

27
I'M PREGNANT

Sometime after I transferred, I fell pregnant with my first child. A 'love baby' I say because although Grant and I didn't plan to be pregnant with our first child when we did, she arrived because of our love and was meant to be. I was ecstatic about being pregnant. However, that excitement soon wore away when I thought about my work. My over-thinking kicked in and it reignited the fear.

- How will work react to my pregnancy?
- I was sure the bosses would be mad as I hadn't been at this station for long.
- Are they going to regret they even accepted my transfer now?
- I worried my supervisors would assume being pregnant meant I wasn't a good worker, and I was worthless and useless in the office.

To say it terrified me to tell work was an understatement. I found out they'd scheduled me to do my yearly pistol shoot whilst I was in my first trimester. You cannot do your pistol shoot whilst you are pregnant, and you state this when you do your pistol shoot. But how will I get out of it without saying I am pregnant? I wasn't ready to tell.

Also, we had a Detective Sergeant from another command come in to help as our Detective Sergeant was off work for a substantial amount of time. Who was the Detective Sergeant who had come in to help out? Detective Senior Sergeant Hart. The same Detective Senior Sergeant Hart who told me I should apply to become a detective, and who also informed me of this detective vacancy position I applied for and was granted the transfer for.

I knew deep within Detective Senior Sergeant Hart would be happy for me and the pregnancy, and there was never any of those patriarchal ideas of running an office when he was in charge. The fear of telling them I was pregnant was still so high. However, deep within, my intuition was telling me to tell Detective Senior Sergeant Hart and everything would be okay.

When I finally built up the courage to tell him I was pregnant, I asked to speak to him in his office when no one else was around. I was shaking uncontrollably, tears were streaming down my face, and my voice was so shaky and squeaky I am sure I sounded like a mouse. "I'm pregnant," I blurted out, followed by, "I'm so sorry. I know I have not been here long. But I promise I will still work hard. I will not be useless. I have been so scared to say anything in case everyone here would be angry at me."

"Stace," Detective Senior Sergeant Hart said, "you don't need to be sorry. This is great news, and I am sorry that you were so scared of telling us. Congratulations."

That sigh of relief. The weight lifted off my shoulders and the fear faded away.

Funnily enough, when I was pregnant with my second child, Detective Senior Sergeant Hart was back at our station again helping out because of low staff numbers. Again, they'd scheduled me to do my pistol shoot whilst I was in my first trimester. During one of my meetings with Detective Senior Sergeant Hart I said, "Since we're in your office together with no one else around, I wanted to let you know I am pregnant."

Detective Senior Sergeant Hart said with a smile, "First off, congratulations. Secondly, I'm glad you didn't apologise for being pregnant. And thirdly, I am glad this time you didn't tell me crying, and didn't make a pledge to do more work because of it."

"Thanks, boss. I am glad I am not doing that this time too," I replied.

THE INTUITIVE DETECTIVE

When I was pregnant with the twins, Detective Senior Sergeant Hart retired. Telling my supervisors at the time I was pregnant with twins went with ease. There was no fear, just love, and that is how it should be for every pregnant working woman.

28
RETURNING FROM MATERNITY LEAVE

After each pregnancy, I returned to work the January after the year they were born. This gave me six to eight months off work on maternity leave. As much as I would have loved to have more time off work, financially for us, it wasn't possible. Whilst I was at work, I needed childcare, and getting a childcare spot near where we lived was hard. If I got a spot at the start of the year, we took it, and since we must pay for the spot, then I may as well be at work and use my annual leave for family holidays.

Each time returning to work after maternity leave had its own challenges. I wanted to show how even though I was a part-time detective, it wouldn't affect my work. I was again trying to show how I was still a hard worker, a dutiful soldier, a good girl, still striving and pushing herself to show she wasn't useless by working part time.

I returned to work, and my workload – like most other part-time police detectives I know – was the same amount of work, if not more, than a full-time detective. Why? Because we want to show that we can be both a mother and a detective. That we can do it all in this patriarchal environment.

I put a lot of pressure on myself when I returned to work after maternity leave. Making sure I was up to date on any law changes and up-to-date learning any new procedures that had come in. I remember every time I came back from maternity leave, the process to apply for an Apprehended Violence Order had always changed. Half the time you didn't know any changes occurred until you were trying to do something, only to be told, "Oh yeah, there is a new way to do that now. You do x, y and z."

When I came back from maternity leave after my first and second child, within a month I was crying in the locker room. A mini breakdown in a way. The pressure I put on myself to try my best, to do it all and show I wasn't useless became too much for me. I feared making a mistake in case it helped people's belief that being a part-time worker makes you useless. What I needed to do was trust myself without the added pressure of other people's perceptions. I had the knowledge. I knew the work. I needed to be gentle and kind to myself.

I was determined to avoid having a mini breakdown at work after I had the twins. I'd specifically spoken to my supervisor as he was aware of the mini breakdown I had when I returned after having my second child. I was very firm about not wanting a repeat of a mini-breakdown and put strong boundaries in place for myself. Knowing these boundaries were acts of love towards myself.

It can be hard coming back from maternity leave. Office dynamics change whilst you are gone, and it changes again when you return. You want to do it all, show you can do it all, and feel negative thoughts about yourself when you feel like you cannot do it all.

When I have this conversation with other women who are coming back from maternity leave and they are worried about trying to do it all, I ask them, "Who's validation is it you are wanting? Deep down, under the layers, whose validation are you wanting and why? Check to see if your response is out of love or out of fear"

29
ALLANAH

When my eldest was four, and my second child was two, my youngest sister, Lisa, was pregnant with her second child. Lisa was a single mother, and throughout the whole pregnancy she wasn't only excited about the impending arrival of her daughter, she was excited her son was becoming a big brother – and at four, he was excited himself. My sister gave birth to the most perfect little girl called Allanah. She was a tiny baby at five pounds and already possessed an unlimited amount of strength.

My sister and Allanah were in hospital for several days and when they arrived home, my sister was so excited to be home with her children.

On the seventh day of Allanah's life, everything changed. I was playing outside with Grant and my two girls when my phone rang. Mum was calling. I felt something was wrong. My stomach was in complete knots and felt heavy. I didn't know what was wrong, but knew she had bad news to tell me.

"Hello," I answered.

"Stacey!" Mum screamed. Her scream had panic, fear, and upset all in one.

"What's wrong, Mum?"

Mum cried inconsolably.

"Mum, what is wrong? Where are you?"

"It's Allanah. She is hurt. Stace, she is not looking good. We aren't sure whether she will make it," Mum said in between her cries.

The knots in my stomach changed to an instant stab. The intensity was overwhelming. "I don't understand, Mum. What happened to Allanah?"

A Detective attached to the Child Abuse Squad spoke on the phone and told me Allanah was at hospital with my sister, and my mum was with my nephew where arrangements would be made to obtain some statements.

I told the officers I was making my way to the police station as a support person only, and not in affiliation with my position as a police officer, before I hung up the phone.

I still didn't have any idea what was happening. All I knew was Allanah was seriously injured and the consensus from the police was that my sister was the person responsible. Grant made arrangements for babysitting our children so he could head to the hospital, and I headed for the police station. As I sat in my car ready to go, I closed my eyes, took a deep breath and said to myself, "Will Allanah be okay?" I intuitively felt the answer was "Yes." I then asked myself, "What could have possibly happened?" I intuitively knew whatever happened wasn't from an intentional act and was an accident. This wasn't what I'd *hoped* was the case. This was what I *knew* was the case.

I called Lisa on the way to the police station and found out Allanah was going into surgery. Lisa said as she was breastfeeding her every three hours, she had Allanah in the bassinet next to her bed. When my sister woke around 6 am to feed Allanah, Allanah wasn't in her bassinet. Panicked, my sister jumped out of bed, she ran out of her bedroom door and found Allanah on the bathroom floor.

After calling an ambulance, they took Allanah to the local hospital. Allanah was having seizures. They then transported her to the children's hospital where they placed her on life support.

> *Spending time at the police station with my mum and nephew, there was a lot of energy, a lot of talk about the possibility Allanah would die. Mum wanted to desperately go to the hospital to see Allanah in fear she would pass away before we could get there, however, the police were adamant on obtaining statements first.*

I intuitively knew Allanah would be okay. I knew she wouldn't die while we were at the police station. I knew it within me, I felt it within me, and this left me feeling calm in what was a stressful and traumatic event.

30
TURN OFF THE LIFE SUPPORT

The next twenty-four hours were surreal. There was a meeting with doctors as they detailed to my sister and Allanah's father the extent of her injuries. Which was – my niece was on life support and they didn't expect her to survive. These doctors believed if Allanah was to survive, she would be severely disabled, deaf, and have no ability to walk or communicate. These doctors suggested we all say our goodbyes and turn off the life support where Allanah would die. On top of that there were Homicide, Child Abuse Squad and the local police detectives investigating how my niece got seriously injured and if they deemed my sister responsible, the charges that could be laid varied whether my niece survived.

My sister responded, "My daughter has not been here for less than twenty-four hours and you're already giving her the death sentence. I am saying no to turning off the life support at this time." All the doctors in the room nodded in agreement to her decision and left the room.

As I walked out of the room with my sister, she looked at me and said, "I know all these doctors here think I did something to Allanah. I see how they look and treat me. I don't know if they will all see the truth that I didn't hurt her. But I know that Allanah will not die. See that board?"

I looked up and saw a big notice board on the wall in the walkway.

"When Allanah was in surgery when she arrived, I walked over and looked at this board. It has pictures of babies that have been in here in the NICU who survived whatever it was that led them to be here in the first place. And I know Allanah's picture will be on here too."

Hearing the doctors say they believed Allanah had no chance of survival felt different. As if it was happening in another world. Every time I would look at them, I felt as if my eyes were questioning their skills as a doctor. I intuitively knew she would survive. Why didn't they?

31

WARRIOR

Within twenty-four hours of the doctors saying they should turn off Allanah's life support as she would not survive, Allanah was improving, and she started breathing on her own. Because hitting her temple gave her new and little brain seizures, her head swelled up. As the swelling went down, Allanah started responding well, which meant they took her off life support. Allanah showed, at just over one week old, how much of a warrior she is.

At the time we were celebrating Allanah's achievements, the decisions made by Family and Community Services, otherwise known as FACS, changed the course of everything. FACS took the parental rights away from Allanah's parents. This meant FACS had the overall say on everything that involved Allanah. No one could visit Allanah unless they had FACS approval. And in front view of all of this, there was this gorgeous little baby, who could now be held in NICU, and her parents could not see or be near her anymore.

"This baby needs to be held and told she is loved by so many. Who will do that if her parents can't?" I asked FACS.

"The nurses can when they have time," was the response I received.

That response wasn't good enough for me. I became a certified person with FACS and I went in every day to just hold Allanah in my arms. To have her feel my heart beating against hers and tell her how much she is loved not only by her mother and father, but everyone else including me.

The other question to FACS was, "What will happen to Allanah when she can leave the hospital?"

Grant and I were told, "If she can't stay with family, then she will go to foster care."

Grant, without hesitation said, "Well she's not going to foster care, she will come home with us."

When Allanah was three weeks old, the hospital discharged her, and I walked her out of the hospital myself. I had the same grey baby bodysuit for both of my girls when they were born and came home from the hospital, and Allanah wore it too.

> *As I held Allanah and walked her out of the hospital, I cuddled her up to my chest and whispered in her ear, "You are loved, and you are brave. You, my dear niece, are a warrior."*

32
WELCOME TO OUR HOME

Having Allanah in our care, meant she was also a member of our family, and for that moment we were a family of five. I always said to her I was her aunty, but I treated Allanah as one of my own children. First thing was paying for her to have a newborn photo shoot. I knew my sister wanted newborn photos of Allanah once she was born. I remember her talking about all the different props they could use in the photo shoot with her gorgeous daughter sleeping in the picture. So, I got that done and gave copies to both of Allanah's parents.

Allanah had a lot of specialist appointments whilst she was in our care. Although Allanah was showing no signs of being deaf, blind, and unable to move, she was still under a lot of observation and had different therapies to make sure she was reaching her milestones and help her if she needed it. Allanah was reaching all her milestones. All the tests she underwent showed she didn't have a disability because of the accident. Allanah was a healthy baby girl.

Through this whole time, I was still working part-time hours as a detective and my mum would look after Allanah the three days I worked each week. Grant and I took turns with the early hour feeds, just like we did when our babies were newborns. The times I did the early morning feeds were my time with Allanah that was just the two of us. I held her just like I did in the hospital, stroking her face, and telling her not only how much I loved her but also how much her mummy, daddy and every family member loved her.

As Allanah was reaching her milestones of rolling, crawling, walking, talking, and first solids, I was so excited and so proud of her. I was a proud aunty with the heart and feeling of watching my own child reaching these milestones. And at the same time, I secretly hoped Allanah would not do it first in front of me. Instead, I hoped Allanah would do her milestones for the first time in her separate visits with her mum and dad. They were her parents, and they both loved her so much. They deserved to see the milestones first, and deep down, I felt guilty if I experienced those moments before them. I felt like I was robbing them of their precious memories.

> *I believe Allanah and I have a special connection, a connection that goes deeper than me being her aunty in this lifetime. We have met before, I know it. It is why I believe we have such a special bond together.*

33

TRANSITION

It was becoming evident during our time with having Allanah in our care, that FACS wanted Allanah to live with her dad. Although I was devastated for my sister, FACS didn't want Allanah to live with her. I also knew that Allanah living with her dad was a good thing. He is a great father, and he was *her* father. Having Allanah in my care meant I was the spokesperson for Allanah. And so, my intention throughout the whole time Allanah was in my care was that I acted to what was in the best interests of Allanah.

If FACS wanted Allanah to live with her dad, then I wanted to make it a smooth transition for not only Allanah, but my kids too. I increased days Allanah spent at her dad's house each week, which meant around Mother's Day in 2017, I handed Allanah to her dad for the last time. The last time Allanah was in my care. I knew this was the right step for Allanah. I love Allanah so much but knew her home was with her parents. And in this case, with what FACS would approve, meant it was to be with her dad.

I held Allanah tight, kissed her forehead, and told her how much myself and her parents love her before I handed Allanah over for the last time. I then got in the car with Grant and the girls and Grant drove home. Although I knew this moment was coming, it was still hard to live it. I had tears in my eyes and as soon as I got home. I knew deep down Allanah was where she was meant to be, with one of her parents instead of with me.

I knew my job was to be the aunty that held her during this time so her body could heal and flourish, but I also missed her presence. I also could not think about my sister hurting because Allanah wasn't with her. Because if I was hurting this much, I knew my sister was feeling an indescribable amount of pain and grief.

34
HE'S GONE, HE'S GONE

Over the years, Mum cried and had her sad moments about Dad. I knew she kept her grief about him at a distance from us, believing it was her way to keep a strong face for us kids. After my dad died, Mum didn't date anyone for over ten years until she met a man called Pete. Mum and Pete lived together for seven-and-a-half years. Pete was a school cleaner where he worked shiftwork, working in the mornings before school started and, in the afternoons, when school finished.

Mum looking after Allanah whilst I worked meant for three days a week she stayed over my house for the sixteen months Allanah was in mine and Grant's care. As the time was approaching for Allanah to live with her dad full time, and we were transitioning that process, Mum and Pete organised to do some travelling together once Allanah was in her dad's care.

About a month after Allanah went into her dad's care, Pete became sick. Everyone thought it was the flu, and Pete refused to see a doctor. I was in my backyard with Grant and the girls when I saw a phone call from Mum. When I saw her name on the phone call, I intuitively knew I had to answer this call.

"Hello," I said. As I answered the phone, I felt sick and nauseous. And then I heard it. I heard my mum scream.

I have heard that scream before. That scream was the instant signal to 'shit has gone bad'. It was the scream I heard Mum scream out when she told me to get Aunty Margaret before Robert was born. The scream I always imagined her making when she found my dad dead. The scream when I got the call about Allanah being injured and the scream I'm hearing now.

"He's gone, he's gone," is all I could hear my mum as she was screaming and howling into the phone.

"Mum, what's happening? I don't understand."

"Hello, is this Stacey? Are you her daughter who is a police officer?" said an unknown female voice.

"Yes," I answered.

The female on the other end of the phone told me she was an ambulance officer and before she could say more, I interrupted and said, "Are you going to tell me that Pete has died?" I don't know what made me ask this. It was just a knowing within me that Pete was no longer with us in physical form.

"I'm sorry to say that he has died," the ambulance officer replied.

Mum got on the phone, and she was crying. I told Mum I was coming right over. Grant was on his way home from work, so I organised to drop the girls off at a family member's house so Grant could pick them up on the way home.

When I got to Mum's house, the police were already there. They'd cordoned off the house whilst they did their investigations for the coroner. I did my best to just be there for my mum.

Mum told me how Pete came home from work earlier that morning complaining of a sore back. It was so bad, he had to be driven home by colleagues as he could not drive himself. Mum said she wanted to take him to the doctors, but Pete refused saying he needed to sleep off the flu he believed he was getting. Mum had arranged to take a friend who didn't drive to do her groceries. When she told Pete she would cancel it to make sure he was okay, he again told her not to worry and to go take her friend shopping as he would just be sleeping, anyway. When Mum got home a couple of hours later, she found him unresponsive in the hallway.

Before the government contractors took Pete to the coroner's, Mum spent some time with Pete to say goodbye. I was standing in the kitchen, which was at the end of the hallway, and saw Pete's lifeless body lying on the hallway floor. Someone placed a sheet over his body, just exposing his head. I could see the medical equipment protruding from the sheet they'd used to defibrillate him. I looked at Pete's face. Although his face looked peaceful like he was asleep, I could tell he was dead.

Mum was on her knees crouched over Pete. She held his hand with one hand and patted his head with the other. Mum kept saying in between the tears, "Why did you leave? Why is this happening again?" Mum held her head to Pete's head as she sobbed whilst she again said, "Why did you leave? You were not meant to leave me. Why is this happening again?"

> *I saw my mother broken. My heart was aching as I could see and feel her in pain from grief. The feeling was so overwhelming, and I'd never experienced it before, and I realised it was because I'd never seen my mum in this raw emotional state before. With Dad's death, I could tell Mum was keeping things together, trying to be strong for us kids. But here, I saw her let that wall down, and her emotions were raw and unapologetically out.*

35
MESSAGE RECEIVED

After watching my mum say goodbye to Pete as he lay dead on the hallway floor, they took Pete to the coroner's. My sister Lisa stayed with my mum, so I left to drive home. Being alone in the car gave my mind a chance to debrief over what had just happened.

As I was driving home, I thought about my mum and how broken she was.

"Why is this happening again?"

Those words were on repeat in my mind. Not only has my mum come home to find both her partners deceased, she's had to make the 000 phone call to emergency services for assistance. She's had to try to revive both of them even though she knew their life had already ended on this earth as she didn't want to believe it was the case. And she's had to hold their hands and ask, "Why did this happen?" She's had to say goodbye.

Was I meant to see this side of Mum? Was this to heal the mother wound?

That's the thoughts that were on my mind.

SMASH.

As I come to, I realised I'd been in a car accident. How?

It turns out as I drove 50 km on a straight road, a young female who was a P plater driving another car turned out of a small side street onto the road I was driving on. She t-boned me right into me.

I could not open my driver's door. The impact was too severe, so

THE INTUITIVE DETECTIVE

I exited through to the passenger side. Still so perplexed how a car hit me, a young female driver greeted me. She was upset, with tears streaming down her eyes over the car accident.

Back into police mode I went. "Are you okay? Are you hurt?"

"I'm fine. I am just so sorry I hit you. I don't understand, I know it's nighttime, but your car is silver, and I just didn't see you until I hit you. Oh my God! Look at your car," she cried.

"The great thing today is that no one was hurt. Mistakes happen. Cars can always be replaced. People can't," I said.

"Why are you being so nice? I have ruined your car. I must have ruined your day," she said.

This poor young female hung her head down in a defeated stance. I could feel she was feeling shame and guilt and she was in her own low vibrational feeling.

"Because nothing positive comes from being an asshole. We all make mistakes and if you are going to have a car accident ever in your lifetime then this is the perfect car accident to have. You haven't ruined my day," I replied.

I eventually made it home. I sat down on the couch.

Wow, what a day. I could not have pictured any of this happening when I woke up this morning.

And I again thought back to witnessing my mum holding Pete this afternoon. The flashback of that vision is as strong in my mind now as I write this, as it was the day I witnessed it. This was a side to my mum I'd never seen before. Was I meant to see that side of Mum? Has witnessing this healed the mother wound between us? Well, if being hit by a car just after I first thought that question wasn't a definite yes, then I don't know what would. Don't worry universe, I received this message.

> *What was the message? It was that I was meant to see this different side to my mum. How a strong woman, with wisdom and lived experience, was sitting in her sadness and grief. Breaking down my beliefs of my mum and seeing her raw side with no judgement. Any leftover frustration or anger I felt towards my mum seemed to have vanished.*

I have felt I was always the person who gets called when something goes bad, where I come in to get control of the situation. But not this time. My job wasn't to fix or help her. It was to create the safe space to allow her to sit in this moment.

36

I GUESS WE'RE NOT BUYING THAT CAR TODAY?

Grant, the girls, and I were in our new house. I was off all the medications from my back injury. I finished exercise rehab and was back to normal exercise. My work on loving myself was going great. I felt like I was in a great place mentally and physically. I then started getting so tired that I was falling asleep by 7 pm most days. I intuitively knew I was pregnant. But all pregnancy tests kept saying negative.

"Maybe you're not pregnant then?" said Grant.

"I'm pregnant. I know it and I can feel it. The tests are wrong," I replied.

From the day my period was due (which ran like clockwork) until ten days after my estimated period date, I took a pregnancy test and every day those tests were negative. I bought so many pregnancy tests and different brands, but they all said negative. On the eleventh day, there it was! A positive pregnancy test.

I scheduled an ultrasound to be done when I would be roughly eight weeks pregnant. During this time, we'd decided to sell our car and buy another car to cater for our new baby arrival. Grant researched for four weeks before he found the car he believed was perfect for us. We just needed to test drive it and see it in person.

Perfect! On the Saturday we have our ultrasound, so we can go there, then straight after it go to the car yard to test drive this car and go from there. The girls were with us for the ultrasound. Both not caring at that point that we were having an ultrasound because they were becoming big sisters.

The sonographer placed the gel on my stomach, and he started moving around his Doppler. The screen for seeing my baby was still facing him. So, I was looking at his face instead until I could see. His eyes widened, and I instantly felt relieved. I could tell from that alone he'd found the baby and a heartbeat.

The sonographer turns the screen towards me and says in a serious tone, "What do you see?"

"There's my baby," I said pointing to a small speck I could see in a sac on the screen.

"What do you think that is?," he said pointing to the bottom of the screen underneath it.

I knew deep within if he was asking me this, it was because there was another baby. But I didn't believe myself. I second guessed myself and said, "That's my bladder?"

"No, that's not your bladder," he said, followed by a little smirk. "That's another baby."

"What?"

"You're having twins," the sonographer said.

I could not believe it. I thought he was playing a trick on me. "No way," I said laughing and holding my hands to my mouth. "Really? Are you playing a trick on me?"

"No tricks," the sonographer replied. He then placed the Doppler over the sac I'd pointed out, turned on the audio, and said, "This is Twin A."

There it was, we were hearing a baby heartbeat.

The sonographer then moved the Doppler towards the sac I thought was my bladder and said, "This is Twin B."

And there it was again. A separate heartbeat.

I looked at Grant, stunned. He hadn't said anything yet. To be honest, he looked speechless. He could not stop staring at the screen. And finally, he put his words together to say something.

"I guess we're not buying that car today."

I like to believe that before we're conceived, we get to choose who our parents will be. To help us with whatever our purpose is to be during that life. The same goes to our children, believing they chose us to be their parents before they were conceived.

And with that theory in mind, I believe my second twin had a few choices to pick as her parents and chose Grant and I after seeing what we did with Allanah.

37
HEARING A SCREAM WHEN NO ONE SCREAMED

The moment arrived. My twins turned one. The first year was such a challenge too. Not only juggling two babies, but juggling motherhood of four children, a career, and a husband who was hating his job. Everything with life throughout the twins' first year always felt like life was keeping me on my toes. Challenging me in more ways I didn't even think could challenge me.

The twins' first birthday was an exciting moment. With each of my children, including Allanah when she was in our care, I created a backyard birthday party and made a cute little outfit for them to wear. I am not very domesticated when it comes to baking, or cooking, but I do know how to sew.

Our closest friends and family came to help us celebrate the twins' first birthday. The day was going great. The sun was shining, there was so much food, and the kids were all playing in the backyard, filling the air with laughter.

Behind our back fence is bushland with a large nature strip in between allowing more area for the kids to play. In that area were swing sets, a tree house, and a netted trampoline where the kids all played.

It was time for the pinata. Grant hung it up on the tree in our backyard and I went inside the house to get some empty paper bags so all the kids could put in their lollies they'd receive from the pinata.

I was standing in my dining room talking to a friend, informing her the pinata was about to start in the backyard when I stopped mid-sentence. I dropped the bags on the ground and ran to the back door. All I knew inside me was that a kid was in trouble. I didn't know any details. I just knew I had to get outside. I got to the back door, and I heard it. I heard a scream. A child's scream. To me, this scream was so loud and blood curdling. The scream I heard was because something was wrong.

I opened the back door and ran down the stairs yelling, "Who screamed? What's wrong?" and to my surprise, all the parents and kids in my backyard acted like nothing had happened. Parents were sitting eating, the face painter was still painting kids' faces, kids were running up to the food table and grabbing snacks to eat. It was like they didn't hear the scream at all.

I ran down the stairs towards the bushland. I yelled, "Didn't you hear the scream?" with everyone's responses saying, "No, Stace there was no scream."

I ignored them all and continued running towards the back of my yard, out where the swing sets, tree house, and trampoline was. I knew something was wrong, but I wasn't sure what. I know I heard a scream.

I ran towards the back fence, and it was then I saw kids running to me. My eldest daughter ran up to me.

"Mama, Willow has hurt herself in the trampoline."

As I ran past her, I told her, "Go to Dad, please."

I ran to the trampoline and there was Willow. Willow was a ten-year-old girl, a family friend. I have known Willow all her life as I have been friends with her mother all my life. I got to the entrance of the netted trampoline, and I could see Willow lying on her back. Her head tilted to look at me, and there it was. Willow had broken her tibia, the bone between her knee and ankle, and it was as clear as day. No bone was protruding through the skin, but the bottom of her foot was hanging.

"I'm here, I'm coming."

Climbing in, I saw a pink ball the size of a soccer ball, which I threw out to stop it from rolling into us. It turns out that ball somehow landed in the trampoline when Willow was jumping. Willow landed on the ball, slipped, and broke her leg.

I grabbed her leg where I could see the break was. I held it in my hand to stop her foot from hanging and used my right hand to balance on the trampoline. My hand became her splint. Grant came behind me along with other parents, who were coincidentally all police officers. Grant and the police officers all went to work. Calling an ambulance, getting things to make a sling, and distracting the other children with them, playing the pinata. I turned to Willow.

Me: "Hello baby, are you okay?"

Willow: "I'm okay. I'm scared."

Me: "It's okay to be scared. Are you in pain?"

Willow: "I was, but how you are holding my leg means I don't feel it as bad anymore."

Okay, I cannot move my hand at all so Willow can't feel the pain. I wanted to alleviate any pain as much as I could for her.

Me: "I'm here, and I will keep holding your leg this way until the ambulance arrives, okay?"

Willow nodded in agreement.

Me: "Just keep looking at me and before we both know it, an ambulance will be here soon. You are doing a great job Willow."

Willow: "I'm so glad you are here Aunty Stacey."

Me: "I wouldn't want to be anywhere else. I love you very much."

Willow said she wanted to look at my face as that made her calm, and so that is what I did. I wasn't there to fix her injury. I was there to hold space for her by allowing our nervous systems to connect so they could co-regulate. Willow is a strong, resilient, and powerful young lady. She knew what she needed to help her. I just followed her cues.

Willow at the time states she didn't scream when she broke her leg. She told the surrounding kids to get help. My eldest along with other children at the party said they didn't hear Willow scream either, only Willow asking to get me and her parents, who were at the party too.

After Willow and her parents left in the ambulance to go to hospital, people were coming up to me.

"Stace, I've never seen anything like it. You just knew someone was in trouble before anything even happened."

The thing is I did hear something. I heard her scream. Even if others didn't hear it, I did. I heard the vibration of Willow's scream. My intuition was speaking to me, and I was listening.

Due to COVID restrictions and lockdowns our state had, we did not have a party at our house for nearly 2 years since the twins' first birthday.

In the lead up towards the first birthday party after COVID restrictions and lockdowns I was feeling a lot resistance and frustration to host another birthday party. In reflection, during some breathwork when sitting in silence by myself, I realised I was feeling the resistance and frustration within my body. I was anxious and worried another child would get injured at one of our birthday parties. When I realised that, I continued doing the work within me.

Breathwork, EFT Tapping, and journaling help me flow through the feelings of trauma I needed to release from my body. Making the choice to go into the next birthday leading with love and not in fear.

PART 4

WAKING UP TO MY POWER

38
YOU HAVE A VOICE

You may know someone, or it maybe you yourself, who knows how to use their voice. Growing up, the person I knew who used her voice was my mum. Mum was a seamstress, and she sewed clothing for well-established and big companies. Not only did she sew my costumes, she also sewed other people's costumes for their solo routines. For our troupe costumes, our dancing studio had a seamstress they liked to use before they had them made overseas. My mum, strong in her belief and ability, refused to pay for someone else to sew a costume when she could, and did a great job herself.

When it was time to get into a new costume for the reveal in class, we would all stand in line so the teacher could have a look at everyone's costumes. She'd make sure they fit properly before we danced the routine.

With the other girls' costumes, if there was anything that needed changes, it was always just a quick little whisper to the seamstress on what the alterations needed to be. The seamstress would write it down in her book and then they would move on to the next person.

When it was my turn to have my costume looked at, I felt like I was always different to everyone else. They went over my costume with a fine-tooth comb, and I felt the energy of the teacher being ready to pounce on my mum for any imperfections they perceived there to be. If anything needed to be altered/fixed with my costume, you can bet your bottom dollar not only would the imperfection be pointed out, but everyone would hear about it in the class. When they questioned something on my costume, my mum was ready to speak up for herself if needed. Sure, sometimes Mum would respond happily to the constructive criticism and fix any changes needed. But if it were something my mum felt was more on an attack to her and not about the costume itself, she would speak up. And every time she spoke up, I would cringe. I felt embarrassed and ashamed that more attention was being drawn to me.

What I didn't realise until years later, was what my mum was unknowingly teaching me. Mum was teaching me you don't have to be little, you don't have to dim your light, you don't have to be the good girl, and you don't have to have validation from others. You can use your voice, you do have strength to stand up for yourself, to stand your ground with conviction, and to radiate your glow.

> *Honour yourself, speak your truth, shine your light. Because liberation is knowing you are not here to make everyone else comfortable.*

39
NOTHING NEEDS TO BE FIXED THERE

My introduction to society standards of how female bodies should be was dancing during puberty. I'd been doing jazz, tap, ballet, and modern contemporary dancing since I was three years old. By the time I reached puberty, my body had become the focal point of conversation for most of my dance teachers. I wasn't a slender and petite teenager. I was an average weight, had thick thighs with strength, was curvy all over, and the extra thickness of myself would mean I would need a size bigger at times to accommodate my body comfortably. By society's standards, I didn't fit in a traditional dancer's body. Add in being the odd person in the group, being a redhead and with the acne that came with my puberty, I wasn't the 'ideal' dancer I believed some dance teachers desired. But in what should be normal standards, I had a traditional dancer's body as I was a soul in a body and used that body to make movement.

During my time in puberty, I felt the thin bodies were always at the front and centre. The appearance of dancing was more important than the dance and movement itself. Every now and again you would see a full-figured and curvy dancer at the front, mainly to the sides. And of course if it were a dance routine to depict a character that was full-figured, otherwise it felt like we just helped make the stage look full.

One costume I wore for a dance routine was a crop top and tight pants which exposed my stomach. Again, they inspected my costume when the teacher said to my mum, "Stace needs to wear fake tan when wearing this costume. She is getting a bit fluffy in her stomach area. That needs to be fixed."

"Nothing needs to be fixed there," my mum snapped back. "Stace is perfect just the way she is."

I think the teacher realised what they'd said as the teacher stopped talking to my mum and walked to the next person to inspect their costume. I was so proud of my mum for standing up for me, yet the fear of being judged by others quickly overshadowed me. My intuition was embracing this moment in hopes to help guide me to loving my body, yet I was so consumed on being judged by others, it embarrassed me. I didn't want my mum to 'make a scene'. I just wanted to fit in. I thought getting validation from others in the hopes I would 'fit in' and 'be accepted' was more important than my beliefs and authenticity.

As I was in the car with Mum on the way home after that, I asked her, "Am I fat?"

Mum said, "No, why do you say that?"

I said, "Because the dance teacher said my stomach was big."

Mum said, "First thing is, you are not fat. That teacher should not have said that."

I said, "But I am not stick thin. I don't have a dancer's body. I have red hair. I am just so different to everyone. I don't like it."

Mum said, "Why does stick thin have to be a dancer's body? Your body of thickness, strength, and curves is inherited from my European genes and so is your red hair. You may not see or realise it now, but being the same as everyone else is boring. You were never meant to be boring. You are different for a reason. You are perfect just as you are."

> *To any person at any age, I say to you; Your body does not equal your worth. In fact, you are so much more than your body.*

40
RELEASING THE GUILT

As the years passed from being a teenager into an adult, I was very self-conscious of my body and thinking I was too fat. I hated the colour of my red hair for always being so different. It was a never-ending battle with loving my body. As a teenager, I bullied myself on my thoughts about my body, believing I wasn't worthy and not lovable. I was using over-the-counter diet pills daily like lollies in hopes I would get miraculously skinny overnight. Believing I would only be absolutely loved if I were how I believed society portrayed women who got everything in life—skinny and gorgeous. I hated showing my legs and would wear jeans on the hottest of days. I even wore jeans to the beach and would refuse to get into the water. Instead, I opted to be the bag lady. In fact, I always offered to be the bag lady as an excuse not to be in swimwear and be in the water.

After having my second daughter, the self-conscious thoughts about my body continued as I went through two pregnancies in less than two years. Everything appeared great on the outside, but on the inside, I was fighting with myself over my body. Facing the inner conflict of trying to appreciate what my body had already gone through, yet frustrated, upset and angry that I didn't 'bounce back' after pregnancy.

I avoided photos of myself, because every time I saw a photo, I would look at it and pick all my flaws and think how disgusting I looked. Seeing that photo, to me, made me believe my day was ruined. I was unhappy and sad for the rest of the day, embarrassed for my looks and believing I was unlovable.

With two children under two, I did baby wearing. I would have my second child in a baby carrier or wrap, have my eldest child sitting in a trolley, and off to do grocery shopping I went. Having the baby carrier made me feel somewhat secure about myself. A baby carrier and a baby inside covered my entire front. I felt it was the best way for no one to see the flaws I believed my body had with stomach rolls, cellulite, and stretch marks.

Grant was working a lot, and I was feeling overwhelmed with being a mother of two and working. I was withdrawing from my friends and would cancel on catch ups at the last minute. Grant even sent me away to a hotel by myself for the night just so I could have some time to myself.

When my second child was two, I was organising some new updated photo frames in the house, and I realised there was no photos of me and my second child together whilst she was a baby. I'd either hidden them and never displayed them or deleted them all because I felt so ashamed of believing I looked horrible.

I wanted to change the beliefs I had about myself. But the first thing that would always come up was feeling guilty. Feeling guilty for feeling unworthy, unloved, fat, and ugly.

What do I do now? How will I get past this?

The answer I felt was, "Forgive yourself."

I sat in front of my mirror in my bedroom and looked at myself. This was the first time I'd ever looked at myself in the mirror separate to doing a quick mirror check before leaving the house. In this instance, I really looked at myself. I saw a tired me. An emotionally exhausted me. A tired me for being so hard on myself and my body. And as I kept looking at myself, I then said, "I forgive you," and started crying.

I did this every day for a few weeks at least. I cannot remember how long. But I did it every day until I could say, "I forgive you," and not cry.

Why was I doing this to myself? I was forgiving myself for the guilt I had over the way I felt about myself. The crying wasn't only my body releasing the negative energy out, but it was allowing it to flow through me so I could release it. Releasing the trauma I'd stored in my body about my body confidence, helped release the guilt.

Embarking on my self-discovery journey to loving myself and

self-worth, started me on the path of disregarding the limiting beliefs and changing my thought process on myself. I realised that I, and everyone else, are perfect just the way we are.

> *I have one family photo of Grant, our two girls, and myself, when my second child was born. When I embarked on my self-discovery and self-worth journey, I placed that picture in a photo frame and it has been hanging in our house ever since, out of love.*

41
TRAUMA IN MY BODY

The busyness of caring for my family, the family law court matter with Allanah and FACS, Allanah transitioning to her dad's care, working on loving myself, Pete's death, and my car accident – all whilst still working throughout it all as a detective – meant my body hadn't healed. It hadn't a chance to process everything that happened as I knew I needed to be there for everyone else. My body had stored the trauma, and I was avoiding it. In my efforts to work on loving myself, my body, too, was working on releasing the trauma. In my instance, it was releasing the trauma through back pain.

I believe my car accident was the end and beginning to a lot of things. It re-enforced to me just how my intuition led me to watch, and realise how much my mum was storing her trauma, her grief of both my father's and Pete's deaths. I believe it was also something for the other driver who hit me to experience and receive a lesson through. And I also believe it was a lesson for me to acknowledge I needed to give myself and my body a chance to grieve after all the emotional trauma it received.

Not long after Allanah transitioned to her father's care full time, I started getting a pain in my back. Was it from working, especially from wearing the gun belt around my waist and sitting down a lot doing paperwork? Was it from the car accident? Or was it from exercise? Inside me told me to get my back pain looked at, but I ignored it thinking it would eventually go away. I was busy with so many things, the excuses I would give myself. I was ignoring my intuition. I again wasn't acknowledging and working on my own needs.

The pain became so unbearable, I couldn't walk. I was on so much pain medication, including Endone, and at one point, I was off work for over a month as I was on six Endone tablets a day. I saw physiotherapists, chiropractors, and osteopaths multiple times a week for treatment where they were all telling me different reasons for my pain. I even ended up in hospital as the pain was excruciating, only to be told to take more Endone. This was the time we were meant to be trying for baby #3. I was feeling defeated, and I felt like giving up.

Grant took me back to the doctors and demanded something be done. That being on this medication wasn't helping and not fixing the problem. I had an MRI, which showed a bulging disc, and it was hitting my nerve endings affected my L4/5. Finally, I was getting some answers. I was told to see a specialist, which I did. The specialist took one look at my form, which stated my occupation was a police officer. Before he even looked at my X-rays, he said my injury was all work related and to put in a Hurt on Duty (HOD) form. When I questioned that he hadn't even looked at my X-rays, he looked at them, told me I needed surgery, and if it were on HOD, I could have the surgery sooner.

"But I want to have another baby," I said to this doctor.

"Oh no, you can't have another baby. Your back cannot handle another pregnancy. No more babies. Put in your HOD and have the surgery."

This whole meeting didn't feel comfortable with me and gave me a bad feeling within my stomach. I trusted my intuition and left. Although I was happy to not see that doctor again, I was still in a lot of pain, and I left feeling more defeated and deflated. I went back to my doctor and vented my frustration on spending money to see that specialist and to give me another option that wouldn't end in surgery. They gave me the option of having an injection in my back and I tried that first.

Getting the cortisone injections in my back was frightening. I remember lying on my stomach in the medical practice, machines all around me. I asked myself, "Am I doing the right thing?" and the knowing within me answered "Yes."

Because of the type of injections I needed, I had to go there twice for injections, four days apart. It meant moving my thoughts from fear of the unknown to making a choice towards a healthier and more mobile me.

I had my injections and commenced my recovery doing water rehab. The recovery took longer than I thought it would. That didn't help me and my impatient ways. But this was my body telling me to slow down, regardless of how busy life was getting. I spent the time recovering and grieving the change of Allanah not being in my care anymore. I cried tears about how Allanah wouldn't remember being in our care. Cried about the great times we had together, the times I cuddled her, telling her how much she was loved and the times she would put her hands up wanting Aunty Stacey cuddles. It was an acknowledgement of all I'd done and gone through the last sixteen months. And spending time with Grant and our two girls. This was my body forcing me to acknowledge my own needs. This was my body releasing its trauma within me, and this was my body's way towards healing my heart.

> *I allowed my body to rest by listening to my body and giving it time to heal. As my body healed, so did my mind. Intuition does not have a time frame to work by. I thought if I avoided my intuition, it would move on to something else, instead it kept coming back in other ways, in deeper ways, to get my attention.*

42
LOVE YOURSELF

Allanah was now living with her dad, I was back to being a mother to two children, and I had my back pain under control. People seemed to think, based on appearance, that my life could go back to normal. Back to the time before Allanah came to live with us. But my life didn't go back to what it was. And to be honest, it never could have. Not only I, but Grant and our two girls, had evolved and grown during those last sixteen months.

When Allanah was in our care, I became a mother again. Although I didn't biologically birth her, I cared, loved, and tended to her needs like a mother would for their baby. And during the time you have a baby, you also try to incorporate some time for you too. Like most mothers, I didn't do that. I felt guilty to even do that. Because I knew Allanah had a mother who loved her so much. I didn't want to take away anything from my sister as she was always and still is Allanah's mother. But by doing that, I failed to care for myself. At that time, there was so much going on with the police investigation, FACS, Allanah's medical appointments, Allanah's visitations with her family, my own children and work. Our family could not all be in one room unless it was FACS approved. And us as a family didn't want to break any rules, and made sure we did everything properly. I thought I could do it all. And to be honest, I didn't want to fail. I felt like I was the backbone. And by doing all of that, I neglected myself. All the work on my body confidence I did after I had my second child went out the window for me as I didn't maintain it. I went back to my fear beliefs of not being good enough. I neglected my mind, my body and my soul.

One day, I took one look in the mirror and realised I didn't like the person looking back at me. I didn't like the physical appearance of me. And I didn't like the mental side of me. I'd been on survival mode in a constant flight or fight for what seemed like forever. My life was on autopilot, repeating patterns and habit reactions. I realised I failed to acknowledge any of my own needs. I was going through so many emotions and one of them was being angry at myself. I spent so much time before Allanah came to live with us on my self-worth and self-love and I didn't continue with it. My feminine energies were unbalanced, and this meant for me, I wasn't taking care of myself. I wasn't nourishing my body with wholesome food. Instead, I was emotionally eating. I wasn't moving my body. Instead, I always making excuses why I could not participate. I wasn't allowing my mind to debrief itself, scared to sit in silence in fear of letting my intuition speak. I wasn't taking time to make myself a priority. I didn't love myself.

I felt lost, and I kept asking myself, "How can I change this?"

My intuition kept telling me, "Love yourself and increase your self-worth."

How am I meant to love myself, and how am I meant to increase my self-worth?

Working on loving myself and increasing my self-worth, by working through a process of healing, was hard. I was an emotional eater and could easily numb myself with food to escape the uncomfortable thoughts about myself and my body. Even when riddled with guilt afterwards, which sent me on a downward spiral of low self-esteem and confidence, it still seemed easier than loving myself.

I also like to be in control, and I felt like it was easier to want to control everything in my life. To me, I felt if things were controlled, then I could eliminate the need for surprises of discomfort and prevent anything bad that may happen. But being in control in this way wasn't done out of love but out of fear. Fear of letting go. Fear of something happening and I would not be supported. The fear of the possibility of relying on someone. Having to use a support network and the fear of either having to accept help or the fear no one will be there to help.

My ego was making me think trying to control things was a good thing. It was its way of trying to keep me inside my comfort zone and its way of trying to keep me safe. Not surrendering my ego meant I wasn't growing. Surprises don't always have to be a bad thing; they can be a great thing, too.

You can be told by so many people and read so many blogs and books you have the power within yourself to change. If you really want to change, you will change. And all of that is true. But when you are in that moment, when I was in that moment, I could not see a way of loving myself. I could not see a way of increasing my self-worth. It seemed impossible.

I again commenced with small steps and started my mirror talk, added a little extra of doing the practice of Ho'Oponopono, which is an ancient Hawaiian practice for clearing negativity. I stood in front of the mirror and said:

- I'm sorry.
- Please forgive me.
- Thank you.
- I love you.

Some days I would cry. Some days I did it through deep breaths. And some days I did it with a smile. Some days I did embodiment and just moved and swayed my body. But I would always look at myself whilst doing it. Look at myself without picking any faults or flaws I believed I had.

If at any time throughout the day I had a negative thought about my body, I would sit in that discomfort and ask myself, "Why do I think that? Is it true?" Really breaking it down and asking myself more questions on why I feel that. In a sense, I was pretending I was in an interview with myself. Asking questions on the offence of feeling negative thoughts about my body. The answers from that would usually go from I look disgusting, because you can see my stomach rolls, I look fat to other people will think I am fat and I don't like myself. I then would say mantras to myself like:

- I am worth more than my appearance.
- I am enough and always have been.

- I am beautiful.
- I will not compare myself to anyone else.
- I will treat my body with love and respect.

I'd repeat these until I sat in my discomfort. It helped me to consciously see myself to work on myself. To break away from the unrealistic expectations of myself and be friends with myself regardless of what part of my journey I was on. If you are friends with yourself, then you will genuinely care for yourself through the good times and bad. This process didn't all happen at once. In fact, it felt like little-by-little transformations. Some transformations I could not physically see, which made it harder for me to acknowledge at the time.

It made me often question myself and realise I'd spent a good portion of my life wanting to be liked, wanting to be loved, and not by anyone specific, but by everyone. By trying to please everyone else in hopes I could get some type of self-gratification, I was losing my authenticity. I wasn't respecting my boundaries, and I was giving my power away.

I realised my moment of true power was when I accepted I wouldn't be liked by everyone. It sounds strange to think a police officer would be worried she wouldn't be liked. It sounds strange to think a police offer would be worried about not being liked. But the change for me was when I accepted that not everyone would like me outside of work. I needed to understand and acknowledge the only priority was to stay authentic to myself and no one else. To face my fear with humility. To meet my fear, sit in my discomfort, and not use any other methods to self-sabotage. And to remind myself with life not being linear, that neither is transformation. It is cyclic, consisting of highs and lows where each one of them contained lessons my intuition was showing me. By working on loving myself, it allowed me to work on increasing my self-worth. And increasing my self-worth also allows me to increase my intuition.

> *Through the lessons my intuition was giving me, I made sure I was checking in on myself daily, releasing what did not serve me, and creating and holding space for myself without judgement. I gave my body time to embody the change, which eventuated in my back pain going away. I gave my mind time to receive the experience, which*

allowed me to accept, be friends with, and love myself through my soul, acknowledging my self-worth. Guiding myself to feel more aligned and congruent.

43

A NEW WAY OF THINKING

I fell pregnant with twins and wow, what a shock that was to me. We tried for one baby and got two. I often get a lot of negative comments for having twins, but I disregard them without even a thought. We were prepared to have Allanah in our care forever, and the possibility of having a third child could have still occurred where we would have four children in our house. So, when I found out I was having twins, there was never a doubt on whether I could handle it. I knew there was always enough love in our household for four children.

Throughout my twin pregnancy, I felt a sense of confidence and empowerment. I knew I had a voice and could use it if needed. I was taking in the miracle of being pregnant with two babies and being aware of all possibilities that could happen without the sense of overwhelm that can come with it.

Being pregnant with the twins was also the start of an uplevelling for me. It woke me up, so to speak. I had a new way of thinking, a new way of doing, and a new way I lived my life. And this happened to all areas of my mind, body, and soul. I established boundaries, I took responsibility for myself, and I became congruent with myself.

Before I fell pregnant with the twins, I'd recovered from my back injury, was reasonably fit, and was body confident. I'd worked hard with my health and fitness and was proud of my achievements towards loving myself.

Being pregnant wasn't a surprise to me, however, having twins certainly was. And one of the main thoughts I had when I thought about being pregnant with twins immediately went to my body size. It went to how big I would get. Now with pregnancy, it is natural to have your body grow to support and nurture your baby/babies growing inside you. But I was taking this thought to another level. I was thinking how horrible it would be. Horrible because I wouldn't have a cute little bump pregnancy. Worried and concerned about getting 'too big.' I was so concerned on society's standards and the wanting of a cute baby bump, I felt I would be unlovable if I didn't have that.

I think all pregnant bodies are beautiful. I would never think negative of another woman's pregnant body, so why was I already thinking the worst of myself?

And that is when I realised I was still adding conditions to myself to love myself. I could only love myself if I had a cute baby bump, show my cute bump with some maternity clothes, and didn't put on too much weight. Because if you put too much weight on, people will comment. And then after I have the twins, well, I must lose a lot of weight at the start. You know, because I had two babies, I should lose heaps of weight and get back to my pre-twin clothes as soon as possible. Wow, I wasn't putting a lot of pressure on myself, was I?

I intuitively knew I needed to change this mindset. So, I established new boundaries, took responsibility for myself, and worked on becoming congruent with myself. I started expressing myself, connecting to myself, and making choices for myself. I fell back in love with myself. Knowing and believing I was more than a physical appearance. This was the start of my consciousness changing. This was the start of my world changing.

My mind changed from wanting to have this cute baby bump whilst still being fit and active to having a baby bump that grew to accommodate growing two babies. I was still active in my twin pregnancy, and I was thankful to have a healthy and problem free twin pregnancy.

After I had my twins, I then went through the post-partum stage. I didn't want to focus on a number and so I didn't weight myself at the hospital. I didn't weigh myself as soon as I got home. In fact, I didn't weigh myself until I was four weeks post-partum. And even when I weighed myself, I wasn't focusing on the number. The number on the scale didn't define me. I was simply curious.

As I continued to work on a healthier me, I exercised and fuelled my body with nourishing foods. I enjoyed the process, something I never explored after my first two pregnancies. I was wearing bathing suits and loving my body. When the twins were three months, I took them to the pools for the first time. I got in and swam with my girls. I didn't hide my body, I embraced it. I was showing my children I was proud of my body. I was proud of my stretch marks, my saggy skin on my stomach, my curves, and my thick thighs. I was proud of me.

It wasn't until after I had the twins I looked at myself from within. I realised I have the power within me to change my feelings. I have the power to change my actions and I have the power to know my worth. To become self-aware, to show compassion, and to acknowledge my truth.

When I faced this fear of, 'I am not good enough', I forgave myself and replaced the fear with love. I forgave myself for the frustration I felt. I forgave myself for the disappointment I felt. And I forgave myself for the grief I felt and replaced it all with love. When I replace the fear with love, I know I am good enough.

Society tells us how we should look like, feel about ourselves and our bodies, and I felt so empowered to throw all of that out the window. To just be me. To love me. By not spending time thinking about how I should 'change' and 'fix' my body because nothing needed to be 'fixed'. I knew my body was perfect just as it was to me, and that left me so much more time to focus on other things.

I don't want my mind to go back to how I was in my 20s, and so it is me who will choose to not go back to that mindset. I have learnt and grown so much since then. It is also the same about my body. I don't want it to return to my pre-baby body. Because my body has gone through so much since then too. I had an amazing opportunity and blessing where my body grew four babies over three pregnancies. My body, like life, is cyclical, where my body will always change. I am worth more than what society says I should. I continued being guided by my intuition. I was loving myself and I was increasing my self-worth.

Every time I vision and meet my younger self, I now don't give her advice. Instead, I walk beside her, reminding her she is worth it, reminding her there is beauty to be found everywhere, reminding her how much potential she has, and how she will see it all unfold out one day. I continue to give my younger self love.

44
SCAFFOLDING

The person who always had my trust and was always a part of my scaffolding and support team was my husband, Grant. Grant and I have gone through a lot through the years. Some great highs and the lowest of lows. We are continually learning, evolving, and growing both as individuals, as friends, as a couple, and as parents.

Over the years, Grant has seen the commitments and responsibilities I have had with my job as a detective, and as supporting other police officers with traumas. I love what I do. I take my job with great pride. I always have high ethics, and he unapologetically and openly loves me whilst actively supporting me. Our big thing throughout the years we have been together is that we openly communicate with each other. I am open with my feelings, and he is open with his. We hold a safe space for both of us to express and respond to each other's emotional needs.

Apart from having Grant, over the past fifteen years of being a police officer, I felt like it was hard to put my trust in someone with my thoughts, feelings, and beyond. It was easy to work with someone out on the truck in the field, on a particular job or strike force and trust them with your life, but to trust them with your soul was something different. I often withdrew, feeling it was easier not to trust anyone then to trust someone and be judged or hurt. I hate big crowds, enjoy my own company, and have an amazing resting bitch face. So I found it was quite easy to avoid people wanting to be close to me who could have been a part of my support team as much as I could have been a part of theirs.

Being a person to help others though, I had no problem with. When I was a Peer Support Officer in the Police Force, I would provide guidance, support, an ear to listen, and do referrals if needed, for other police officers. They trusted me with their information. I was a part of their scaffolding. And outside of work was no different. I was always there to help others, I just never asked for help myself. I was in fear of being judged. I was in fear of being seen as different. I was in fear of being vulnerable. I was in fear of being unlovable. I was in fear of being seen as human.

I realised after helping other people, both police officers and civilians, I was giving out all my supportive energy and it was taking all my mental strength. Mentally exhausted and drained, I again sat in my backyard one day thinking, "What am I doing wrong?" I was so mentally exhausted by trying to help people and felt it was sucking my soul dry. It wasn't them. I had a choice, and I was allowing them to take all my energy. They were in a low vibrational state, and I thought being there in my high vibrational supportive state would help. But I wasn't setting the boundaries, I wasn't putting myself first, and I wasn't listening to my intuition. The answer that came within me was 'Work on your scaffolding.' And that is what I did.

So I faced my fears of trusting people outside of Grant as he is already on my scaffolding team, and I got my support system up consisting of friends, mentors, and practices to help me.

Don't forget yourself. It is not selfish to work on yourself. Working on yourself helps you become a greater person within, which also helps you become a greater person to others. Remember, you have the choice to choose love or choose fear.

When I didn't have my scaffolding and withdrew from people, it was because I chose fear. For me, it was fear people would judge me for needing help because I am the person who is the helper, the rescuer, and the caregiver. Now I have that scaffolding in place, it reminds me I am human, it is okay to seek help from your support team, and I am no different from anyone else. We all need scaffolding.

45
IT'S TIME TO GO DEEPER WITHIN YOUR INTUITION

During COVID, especially when the schools all went to online learning, I was working as a detective and home schooling the girls at the same time. At that stage, the twins were in a phase of constantly fighting with each other too. Grant was following his intuition and studying to change his job. It felt like everything was pure chaos.

When things got so busy between home and work life, I would sit outside in the backyard, have the sun shining on my face with my eyes closed, and sit in the quiet. Different things would happen at different times. Sometimes it would help me get a chance on my outstanding list I would have in my head. I'd listen to the kids giggle whilst playing, listen to the kids fight and argue with each other, and listen to the birds chirping. At other times, I would just sit and see what came up within me.

I was desiring more growth within my life. I wanted more but was unsure what that meant. On one day, when the girls were playing, and the twins were having a nap, I sat outside, closed my eyes, and let the sun shine down on me. As I soaked up the sun's rays and let it warm my body, I felt this knowing inside me and the words, "It's time to go deeper within your intuition," came to me.

This was something I knew I had to do and learn more about, so I started doing meditations, practicing EFT tapping, and working more on my mindfulness. I was drawn to an intuitive health course and thought that was the direction to take to help me focus more on my intuition. As I was focusing on my intuition, I was noticing things were happening within me. It activated my sacred feminine power. So much energy was shifting through me, and I was embracing the wisdom I knew, the unconditional love it contained, the clarity it showed, and the calmness I felt.

The global pandemic woke me up. It showed and reminded me to connect within myself, my innate intuition, and to go deeper. And I was doing all of that. I was shedding. Shedding my identity as it is a perception to other people. As I went out of my comfort zone, I felt the fear, but it wasn't dominant within me. What was dominant was the love. I was uplevelling.

Our intuition develops when we allow ourselves to go through the layers of our growth and expansion.

46
SHIT MAGNET

I used to think it was a curse that I would go to work as a police officer and be busy with jobs that came in. Even when I was off duty, things would happen from witnessing a car accident and helping everyone, people experiencing medical episodes, and stopping a potential robbery. The title 'shit magnet' that would often be thrown around is when you would be extremely busy with work every time you worked as you somehow were 'there at the right time.' If you are on call, you would be the person who would most likely always be called into work. I also would often get the unique, one-of-a-kind jobs. That gave me the label of being the 'ultimate shit magnet.'

What if I saw beyond that? What if the jobs I attended to as a police officer, as a detective, or even off-duty were chosen for me to attend for a reason? A lesson for myself to learn. To help be a part of a message for someone and/or create or hold space for others as they allow their free flow of memory recall to happen and obtain the version of events in the best capacity possible? To help the victim or witness realise they have a voice? For the victims and witnesses to realise their power is within themselves and they could claim it back? To help them realise how strong they are and help me realise how strong I am? To give compassion without judgement. Allowing their fear to be welcomed around me.

Changing my mindset from 'I am a shit magnet' to 'I am a powerhouse' reminded me I have the power. I have the power of my choices and energy. I could agree with people to say I was a shit magnet and succumb to their energy. Or I could choose to disagree with others and remain authentic and true to myself.

47
A STEP FORWARD

I was feeling empowered within myself. I loved work, felt like I was doing a great job with being a mum of four, and wasn't only friends with myself, but loved myself. I'd started meditation, Emotional Freedom Techniques (EFT) Tapping, and mindfulness as a part of my scaffolding and support to continue towards working on myself.

What is EFT? EFT Tapping is is a branch of Energy Psychology and is a stress reduction technique which draws upon mindfulness, exposure, and physical stimulation. EFT helps to address/shift/dissolve stressful emotions, traumatic events, physical pain, unhealthy habits/patterns, and fears/limiting beliefs that may hold you back in your personal life, relationships and/or career. EFT tapping helps to calm the nervous system and offers relief from negative emotions. It restores balance of energy within your body by tapping with your fingers on specific median (acupuncture) points, primarily on your face, upper body, and hands. Basically, EFT is amazing and can be used for everything. And the most amazing thing is you do EFT on yourself.

I intuitively knew by using EFT on myself it would not just limit to myself. My children would watch me do EFT and I was using it with my older children when they felt anxious, scared, etc.

I started helping other police officers with the use of EFT. Sometimes police face a threat which activates their amygdala in the limbic system in the brain. The amygdala assesses the threat and sends a message to the Vagus Nerve to activate the fight-flight-freeze response. At certain times, activating these responses is necessary to prevent themselves or others from being injured/killed. But sometimes after a traumatic event, the fight-flight-freeze response is still active. I started helping police officers with the use of EFT to help regulate their nervous system so they could get out of their fight-flight-freeze response instead of being stuck in those responses.

I was even using EFT tapping with my victims before they went to Court to give evidence. To help calm their nervous system so they could give evidence without the external fears they may have within them. The fears of saying their story again, the fears of being questioned, the fears of the jury looking at them, the fears of any judgement. Tapping helped them release those fears so they could just focus on what they needed to do, to say their story.

When we work on ourselves, the level of its potency intensifies. It does not then just become for you, but for the collective, for others as well. Your service is your medicine. And for me, I believe it was a step towards waking up to my power.

Waking up to my own power was owning my potency.

48
SPIRITUAL CLOSET

It's safe to say, if you have read this book from the beginning, I am somewhat of a spiritual person. I was cautious about coming out of my spiritual closet. I felt being a police officer meant I could not show any type of side of me. It was a thought I put in my head as an obstacle, an excuse to not come out of the spiritual closet. What will people think? What if people judge me? What if people think I was different?

One day, I wrote those questions down on a piece of paper and answered them with automatic writing:

Question: What would people think if I came out of my spiritual closet?
Answer: I don't know. But does it matter what they think?
Question: What if people judged me for coming out of my spiritual closet?
Answer: My spiritual side is a part of me. It is who I am. If someone was to judge me for showing my spiritual side, do I want them to be a part of my life? Does it serve me to have people in my life who judge me for who I am?
Question: What if people think I am different for coming out of my spiritual closet?
Answer: Well, the fact is, I am different. In fact, we all are different. It is what makes us all unique. There is no normal. And if people were to think I was different, then is that really a bad thing? If they judged

me for being different, then I would refer to my answer to the first question.

My intuition was telling me to come out of my spiritual closet. I needed to tap into the power and wisdom. To hold a high vibration and sacred space for others. To become what I consider a sacred leader. Energetically activating others to see their worth and power through encouraging and empowering them.

And with that, I embraced my spirituality and my sacred service. Unafraid to lead I connected, failed, adjusted, unlearned, relearned, evaluated, felt, expanded, and grew. I called back my wisdom, embodied my power, rose above my fear, and became unapologetically me. My world changed as my consciousness shifted.

I called home the highest expression of myself.

49
SACRED LEADER

When things feel tough, hard, slightly out of my reach, overwhelming and stressful, I close my eyes, take a deep breath and say to myself or out loud my mantra of, "I can do this." The times I avoid doing this, my intuition leads me back again.

I have done this a lot throughout my life so far. When I was feeling left out at school, studying exams at school, and studying my science degree. When I left my science degree, went through the police academy, became a police officer, becoming pregnant, and through being a mother and so forth. I would always go back to my mantra of 'I can do this.' Meaning I can do me, whatever that becomes.

I have done this whilst writing this book and acknowledging where the breadcrumbs of my intuition have led me within this life so far. Service to myself and others and embodying the feminine archetypes that speak to me.

I am a warrior,
I am a wild woman,
I am a priestess, and
I am a sacred leader.

Acknowledging and accepting this was difficult. The saboteur archetype within me would dismiss this by saying I am not a leader. The personal expansion and contraction of putting myself out there.

Working on my inner world before birthing it out into the world. Acknowledging I was resisting from the fear and making sure I don't bypass the potential pain and discomfort. I was witnessing my own becoming. That the sacred leader is within me, with strength, courage, and humility in complete divinity.

I see a sacred leader is someone who embodies their truth and power with a high level of awareness and connection to their humility, staying grounded and congruent. A sacred leader also ensures that whilst people are on their own awakening, on their own healing journey, that they maintain their own sovereignty, as they follow their intuition and connect to their higher self. Reminding you that you are already whole and have the answers within you.

As I connect to my inner wisdom, I lead with my holiness. Knowing I am not doing this on my own and knowing I have been on this earth before. I know I have the power to change the world.

I choose to bring in the qualities of my sacred self into any situation.

I am a sacred leader.

50
MY SERVICE IS MY MEDICINE

After the desire of wanting to be hit by a car so I didn't have to go to work, realising this wasn't right, and transferring to another command, I wanted to make sure I was never in that position mentally again. When I would ask myself, "How can I prevent this from happening again?" I felt the answer within me say, "Daily practices."

I wasn't too sure what that meant at first, but I knew it meant doing some more inner work. I continued with affirmations and mantras. I also included some embodiment movement, the inner dancer in me coming out and just moving my body, creating space with my body, and letting myself go. This led into breathing techniques, meditation, journaling, and EFT.

With the busyness of life, some days are better than others. Sometimes I can do these all-in-one days, and at other times it's more of some things over others. This is all dependent on not only family and work life but what I need. Doing all of this helped me continue to connect to my intuition and trust my guidance. My daily practices became my daily devotions.

Somatic movement was something I realised I was doing but didn't have a name attached to it when I first started. Consciously, with intention moving my body, by bringing awareness to my body, helped guide me towards a more balanced nervous system.

Working on my nutrition was a slow process as there was a lot of emotional eating to face. But I do find eating wholesome foods helps my body and mood. I try to be prepared for the days of unplanned overtime, night shifts and getting called out when on call. It took me a long time to work at it, and sometimes I still get caught out, but overall, it is so much better than when I was a Probationary Constable.

Meditation has been great in allowing me to work on sitting in stillness and solitude. It allows me to connect into the higher frequency of my intuition, to go deeper within my intuition and work on my subconscious fears.

EFT Tapping has been a life changer for me. I wished I learned this when I was a kid. In fact, I do tapping with my kids. I have used it to help me with jobs within the police force that have affected my mental health, including my memory of finding Angel deceased.

Journaling was something I used to do as a kid and teenager in high school. When I finished high school and did my science degree, I stopped. I'd thought about restarting when I became a police officer. I thought it would be a good way to get the jobs I attended that gave me any type of emotion I needed to write about out on paper. I mean, as police officers, we write a lot in our police notebooks and police statements, but it is never about our feelings. When I mentioned this to some police officers, they told me not to do it. That it is best not to have anything recorded about your feelings regarding the job, or the job you attend, in case someone uses it against you. And so, I stopped. I took on their conditioning and limiting beliefs as my own. I took on their fear instead of listening to my intuition.

It wasn't until I woke up during the coronavirus pandemic that I took up journaling again. And my goodness, I realised how much I missed it. I forgot how much I loved it. I realised how much I needed it and how it is a great way to let everything out, even if the sentences don't make sense on the paper.

And the final one was breathing. Breathwork is underrated, yet so powerful. The power is always within yourself and breathwork can connect back to yourself. We were born breathing, and breathing is an amazing way to help self-regulate your nervous system out of fight-flight-freeze responses.

Doing my daily devotions has been a great way to maintain and hold a high vibration of energy. To conduct investigations that involve so much emotion such as sexual assaults, including historical and children, and coronial investigations – which may include people being charged – involved such a high level of energy needed in creating and holding space. These investigations and court matters can take years from start to finish, so it is vital to maintain the holding space in an energetic setting. As my workload increased, my daily devotions increased too. I am thankful I have a supportive husband who realises and understands I need to do these things daily. It makes me a better person.

Now, doing all these things doesn't mean I don't need anything else in my life. I need to ensure I have my scaffolding in place, and to make sure I speak up when I need help in any setting. Doing all of this does not eliminate the need to speak to a counsellor, therapist and/or psychologist if it is needed.

There are some police who refuse to accept any professional help. They're fixated on the possibility of having things recorded in their session that could be used against them. It goes back to the limiting beliefs of why some police officers didn't want me to journal to have anything recorded against me either. The fear instilled in them and limiting beliefs that if they seek help, they're not a good police officer and cannot handle the work of a police officer, are real to them. They fear it could come back to hurt them in the future with promotional or transfer prospects.

The story of the elderly male with dementia in which I spoke about earlier in this book shows how I resisted my intuition on seeking help. With the story of Angel, I sought the help of a psychologist through the Employee Assistance Program (EAP) the police offer. Looking back, my intuition was telling me to continue seeking help as I did not have to do everything on my own. I resisted because of the fear.

I know there are parts of my traumas I still need to work on, and I'm doing that. I also know helping others with their traumas has also been helpful to me and my traumas too. Again, my service is my medicine.

I have not mastered everything in life. I am still learning, and to be honest, I will never master everything in life. I should not. That would fuel the perfectionist. I am constantly reminding myself I am human. A human living this soul experience in this body where I experience the highs of happiness, love, joy, and gratitude and the low of lows with fear, shame, and guilt, that can incorporate trauma, limiting beliefs, and conditioning.

51
PATTERNS

With any type of journey I'm on, I know it is important for me to always be reminded with the fact I don't need to be anywhere other than where I am right now. I am to see and feel with all my senses and beyond on this journey.

Throughout my life, both within and outside of the police force, I know I have learnt about and revisited many patterns. I have learnt to go deeper when these experiences have happened. I learnt, grew, and evolved from them. I become a better person to myself, my family, and to all the people I serve because of the lessons I have learnt. With this, it has made me realise death makes life possible and made me realise my spiritual awakening. To not be afraid of death, and instead, continue my path on an emotional healing journey and personal transformation.

We can spend our time hoping and striving to get to our destination and forget or disregard the journey it took to get there. Our cyclic thoughts and emotions throughout the journey mean just as much if not more than the destination. By appreciating the journey filled with hard work, sacrifices, heart aches, celebrations and laughter means we will not take anything for granted when we reach the destination. We live in the present.

I know with my life thus far, I have revisited many patterns. Patterns regarding having a voice, body confidence, self-worth, patience, and more that goes into healing my trauma. To remind myself I am lovable, I am good enough, I am valued and I am worthy. Each of these patterns I revisit, my intuition is asking me to access in a different way and/or go deeper. To go through the layers that help change my beliefs, not just on the surface but also on a subconscious level. By doing this, it helps me to stay in alignment, to be congruent with myself, which then allows me to continue shining my light bright, being magnetic, to continue inspiring and helping serve others.

The patterns I have learnt about myself have risen through listening to my intuition. Some of these patterns I learnt were around death and/or near-death experiences of other people, and some of those experiences were traumatic for me. It is important for me to know those events didn't happen for me to learn an important lesson. Or for me to acknowledge that everything happens for a reason, or for me to feel these experiences strengthened me. My dad didn't have to die by suicide just so I can learn a lesson or be a stronger person. I don't have to learn lessons through trauma. I do, however, have a choice and I have chosen to work on healing from my traumas. To choose the experiences I have from my traumas to help shape the person I am, but know my traumas don't define me.

My story and the work I do solidifies my desires to help others with trauma. Supporting and guiding others to create a life they can cherish by following their intuition as there is life after trauma.

WRITING THIS BOOK

When I was in Year 11, in the beginning phase of my Higher School Certificate, known as the HSC, I came first in English within my school. I loved reading and would often read at home and in the library at lunch times throughout my schooling years. I had dreams and aspirations to write a book of my own but was never sure what type of writer I would be. During Year 12, I lost my first place for English within the school, and I felt I was a failure.

Over the years, the thoughts of wanting to write a book still came up, but I always just disregarded the thought and pushed it away. My saboteur, the negative thoughts came in my head saying, "No one would buy your book. What would you write about anyway?" and "The book would be crap so don't bother." And my ego came in my head too with thoughts saying, "You're busy being having a career and being a mother. Why bother writing a book when the time spent writing a book can be better directed elsewhere?" I thought the idea and desire to write a book was gone.

It wasn't until I had my spiritual awakening when COVID hit I thought to write. To write stories about when I have listened to and disregarded intuition throughout my life. One day, I did just that and I started writing. It all started flowing out of me. Initially, to write to heal, before going deeper. The strange thing was, I didn't question why I was writing these stories or what would happen once I finished. It was a great healing process for me and left me feeling calm. I knew it was what I needed to do, so I just kept writing.

When I'd written a third of this book, I sat back one day and asked myself, "Why am I writing this? Am I doing this to help me?" The answer my intuition gave me, the knowing inside me that responded to the automatic writing I did answered with, "Yes, and it will become a book." I'd denied my intuition on writing a book for so long that it came around another way in hopes I would listen. This time I did.

When the thought of what I'd been writing would become a book, I was calm. I knew it was the right answer for me. I guess deep down I always knew this would be a book. Thinking I could hide behind the not knowing so if it didn't happen, no one would know. To avoid the fear of no one liking my book and the fear of failure.

I conceived this book through love, not fear. There was no stopping this book being birthed now. This book allowed me to stop the armouring in my body and have the emotions pour out, allowing me to acknowledge and fully circulate the content within my body. It has helped me take back ownership of my life. Reengaging the power with my point of view. Teaching me who I am. Knowing I can impact people's lives with my work, my wisdom, and my legacy.

What will be the next stage of my life? What I do know and feel intuitively is I've activated my soul. I know I am called here to be something more in an energetic awakening. The call to something more is me remembering what I promised to bring here within this lifetime. With that, I will continue to embody my devine self in my true power and show up every day with fierce love.

Thank you for reading this book. I hope this book has shown you how intuition played it's part in my life and trauma healing journey so far, and how it plays a part in yours, too. Empowering yourself to be a detective in your own healing journey. To be on your journey of self-acceptance, self-healing and intuition development. To see where the breadcrumbs take you by surrendering to the fear and embracing the uncomfortableness. By choosing to love over to fear as you continue to evolve and grow. Attuning to your intuition allows you to be the detective in your trauma healing journey.

My life is not complete yet. And neither is yours.

ACKNOWLEDGMENTS

Thank you to my amazing husband, Grant. I feel like words cannot express how grateful I am for your support and love. We have always been there for each other, through the good and bad. Thank you for always being so supportive of my ideas without any question. And to my beautiful four children for being ever so patient with me as I not only wrote this book but birthed it into the world. I am so grateful you all chose me to be your mother.

To my mother. What a ride we have been on together so far. You have taught me so much and words cannot show how much I absolutely love you.

To my father. The amazing thing about love, is that love never dies. My love for you is just as strong as it was when your soul left my lifetime, always timeless in my heart. I love you so much.

To my siblings, both alive in this lifetime and beyond. I love you all.

To my gorgeous niece. Thank you for teaching me what true strength really is. You, my dear cuddle bunny as I used to call you, are one determined and courageous warrior soul I know. I know we have a soul contract together and we will always be in each other's lives.

To my mentor and friend, Tina Bruce, words cannot express how grateful I am we've met again in this lifetime. You are a true mentor, and I am forever grateful for your training and guidance. Your support and empowerment truly mean the world to me. We were meant to be in each other's lives. And I am so glad we found each other.

To my teacher, Dr Ricci-Jane Adams, from The Institute for Intuitive

Intelligence, thank you for your guidance, your teachings, and your fierce love. You have changed my life and I am forever grateful.

To my Publisher, Karen McDermott and the team at KMD Books. Our paths crossed in the most devine way and I am eternally grateful. Thank you all for your love, support and guidance in helping me birth this book.

Thank you to my formal and informal teachers, mentors, and colleagues who have helped me become the person I am today.

And last, to my sisters and brothers in blue, thank you for the work you do to help others. Please remember, you assist, guide, and nurture best for the community when you take care of yourself. You are human, and it is okay to acknowledge and receive help when it is needed.

ABOUT THE AUTHOR

Stacey Webb is, first, an imperfectly perfect human being.

Stacey uses her fifteen years of experience in the Police Force, along with her certifications in modalities of intuition, Emotional Freedom Techniques (EFT), breathwork, embodiment and somatic work to continue to support people who are embarking/continuing their trauma healing journey, allowing them to feel connected to themselves as they release fear and trauma from their lives.

www.ingramcontent.com/pod-product-compliance
Lightning Source LLC
Chambersburg PA
CBHW020323010526
44107CB00054B/1953